THE BIBLE YOU DIDN'T KNOW YOU COULD BELIEVE IN

Jeffrey E. Frantz

St. Johann Press

Haworth, New Jersey

ST. JOHANN PRESS

Published in the United States of America
by St. Johann Press
P.O. Box 241
Haworth, NJ 07641
www.stjohannpress.com

Copyright © 2019 Jeffrey E. Frantz

The paper used in this publication meets the minimum requirements of the
American National Standard for Information Sciences—Permanence of Paper
for Printed Library Materials, ANSI/NISO Z39/48-1992

Composition and interior design by Susan Ramundo
(susan@srdesktopservices.com)

ISBN 978-1-937943-50-9

Manufactured in the United States of America

DEDICATION

This book is dedicated to the loving memory
of my wonderful parents,

Tom and Emily Frantz

CONTENTS

ACKNOWLEDGMENTS

Although I've written hundreds of sermons and articles over the years, this is my first book-writing experience. Thinking back on this, there many people I would like to acknowledge and thank.

To begin with, I think titles matter. For the title of my book, which I like a lot, I am indebted to my talented wife, Yvette. I don't know how she did it, but she came up with the title, *The Bible You Didn't Know You Could Believe In*. She also supported me through the lengthy process of finding a publisher. I also want to thank my daughters, Natasha Lindstaedt and Erica Frantz, both University Professors in authoritarian politics and published authors themselves, for their ongoing support and guidance.

For the actual writing of the book, I owe a huge thank you to my good friend, Marion Olsen. During the writing of the book, month after month we met weekly for her to review what I had written. Many of her suggestions were incorporated into the substance of the book. Her knowledgeable insights and feedback were invaluable to me in the writing process.

I want to acknowledge three people who helped shape by learning and thinking over my four-plus decades of seminary training and ministry. Dr. Bernard M. Loomer, one of my professors at the Graduate Theological Union in Berkeley, California, was my mentor, good friend, and one of the most influential persons in my life. A renowned process theologian, his teaching—particularly in the area of process/relational modes of thought—has nurtured and shaped my thinking for a lifetime.

I would also like to thank Marcus J. Borg for his many books on contemporary theology and the church. In many ways, I consider Borg one of the seminal theologians for the progressive church. Lastly, I am deeply indebted to John Shelby Spong and his inspirational voice for progressive Christianity. I not only learned much from his countless books, but also from his dozens of lectures I have viewed on YouTube.

I want to acknowledge three churches I served who helped nurture and support me over my long career as a local church pastor: the First Baptist Church of Palo Alto (Palo Alto, California), the Community Church of Poway, United Church of Christ (Poway, California), and the Miami Lakes Congregational Church, United Church of Christ (Miami Lakes, Florida).

Finally, I am grateful to publisher David Biesel and St. Johann Press (Haworth, New Jersey) for agreeing to publish my book and for the very professional and supportive manner they have interacted with me in the process.

INTRODUCTION

For years now, I've been wanting to write a book on the *believability* of the Christian faith. In the spirit of the recent rise in the church of *progressive Christianity*, the book would seek to present a view of the Bible, God, and Jesus that, simply put, people could believe in. It would be a book not burdened by the constraints of biblical literalism and the fundamentalist/conservative theologies that flow from it.

A word on progressive Christianity. In some circles, the word *progressive* has come to replace the term *liberal*, which in recent years has become a loaded term for conservatives suggesting softness on issues such as poverty, crime, guns, immigration, government expansion, and traditional views on marriage and religion. Progressive Christianity includes a range of views on the Bible, God, Jesus, and the church.

This book is an expression of progressive Christianity where, specifically, I mean:

- Not taking the Bible literally, rather, reading the Bible in light of its historical context and mostly as metaphorical narrative

- Freeing God from the bonds of supernatural theism

- Viewing Jesus not as divine but as fully human

My general thesis is that, at its best, the Bible is believable, which has wonderful implications for those of us who wish to embrace the Christian faith or simply learn from its teachings. However, for increasing numbers of people, the Bible becomes virtually unbelievable the more it is read in a literal manner, as if all of the Bible were somehow the literal, inerrant, and infallible Word of God.

At the outset, we need to recognize that the Bible that has come down to us over the centuries is plagued by all sorts of flaws, inconsistencies, and contradictions. To be expected to accept many of these passages of scripture as *coming from God* poses serious stumbling blocks for many people of faith. I will discuss this further in chapter 2, "The Problem with Biblical Literalism."

For our purposes at the moment, we want to make the point that biblical literalism, as an interpretive methodology, is not adequate to our modern experience as aspiring believers. We also want to emphasize the importance of reading the Bible (1) in light of its historical context (contextually) and (2) as metaphorical narrative and symbolic language.

The only tenable argument in support of literalism and inerrancy is that at every point of writing, interpretation, and editing over the centuries, the biblical authors were inspired by the Holy Spirit, which automatically freed them from error or imperfection. For progressive-minded Christians, this lacks credibility. Simply put: it doesn't make sense.

WHAT IS AT STAKE?

So what is at stake in all of this? If you assume, as recent research confirms, that the Christian church is in decline and has been for decades, there is a lot at stake for those of us in the church. It is not that the church is going to die. Such a claim would be overreactive and more than a little presumptuous. However, at its best, the church—certainly, the mainline church—seems to be at a crossroads (continuing on a path of steady decline) that has been emerging for decades.

This crossroads has wider implications for American culture as well. Indeed, throughout my forty-plus years of ministry, the issue of biblical literalism has been *the* single most divisive element in the larger church. It symbolizes the divide between conservative-evangelical churches (including fundamentalist and Pentecostal churches) and the more moderate-to-progressive churches in the mainline denominations (i.e., Presbyterian, Methodist, Lutheran, Episcopalian, American Baptist, Disciples of Christ, and United Church of Christ). Every year there seems to be an ever-widening gulf between these two generally opposing ways of understanding and presenting the Christian faith. Oftentimes, understandings about God, Jesus, and the scriptures simply do not agree.

Beliefs around social justice concerns such as abortion rights, gay and lesbian rights (same-sex marriage, for example), gun control, the role of government, minimum wage, gender equality, race relations, global warming and the environment, education, immigration reform, campaign finance reform, and international relations tend to be at odds. (Conservative-evangelicals tend to favor a larger military; they also tend to see the United States as the new Israel and, therein, the recipient of special favors in God's sight.)

This divide around biblical literalism is, of course, only part of the church's problem of decline. Across the mainline denominations, experts are struggling to stem the tide. Easy answers are not forthcoming. For those inside the church and Christian faith, we wonder: What's happening to us? What to do? Where to turn?

Any decline of this sort in religious commitment and practice is generally multifaceted. Some experts point to traditional forms of worship, music, and ministry that have simply lost their appeal. Other experts point to changing demographics. Still others say there are too many choices, too many options of what to do on a Sunday morning. No doubt, all of these explanations are true to some extent.

The contention of this book is that, for many, the fundamental problem with the Christian faith is that—too often—it lacks believability. In other words, *how* the faith is presented is increasingly inadequate to the belief needs and expectations of modern American culture. As the intellectual and conceptual world around us has changed and evolved, the church has not always kept up.

As traditional understandings and assumptions about the Christian faith are fading and dying out, a more progressive way of presenting the faith is called for. This is already happening in some churches. While questions on God and Jesus are important and will involve a major portion of this book, the starting point for a more progressive presentation of faith is the Bible: the way we read it, how we understand and interpret it, and the role it plays in our ongoing faith development.

The Bible continues to be *a* primary source for our learning about God and is *the* primary source for our learning about Jesus. In a sense, the title of this book could also have been *The God You Didn't Know You Could Believe In* or *The Jesus You Didn't Know You Could Believe In*. The reason for the current title rests on my view that biblical literalism is itself at the root of problematic conceptions of both God and Jesus. In American life and culture we have to deal with the Bible first in order to then deal with God and Jesus. In addressing this challenge, the starting point is to not read the Bible literally but rather to read it (1) in light of its historical context (contextually) and (2) as metaphorical narrative.

At the end of the day, people are going to believe what they need to believe. Everybody has a life story that, to some extent, explains what they believe and why they believe it. What we believe about the Bible, God, and Jesus usually has much to do with the teaching and example of our family situation growing up and with our early experiences of church.

In my own life story, my family faithfully attended the Fourth Street Methodist Church in Aurora, Illinois. I have vivid memories of Sunday school classes and worship services. However, I have virtually no memory of teachings about the Bible, God, or Jesus, which proved problematic for me as I grew into adulthood and went on to college, seminary, and a career in local church ministry. It is possible that either the teachings were presented in a low-key manner or that perhaps I wasn't able to be still long enough to both listen and absorb them.

In any event, upon entering seminary at the age of twenty-eight, I didn't have much that I needed to unlearn in order to move forward as an aspiring minister. I was simply looking for a seminary education that was progressive and enlightened enough to cohere with my evolving liberal orientation at the time, and I needed the intellectual space and encouragement to continue discovering what I believed. For me, this was a relatively painless time of searching and discovering. I remember seminary being fun, meaningful, and at times exciting.

However, for the majority in our country, childhood and youth experiences of Christianity and church have most likely been traditional and more conservative-evangelical in nature. Where this has not been the case, the overarching orientation in our culture has reflected the more traditional notions of what people mean in our wider community when they say they are Christian.

TRADITIONAL CHRISTIANITY

Generally, when people say they are Christian in the United States, what they mean is some form of general consent to the popular Christianity of our wider culture. A somewhat abridged form of biblical literalism is assumed (most of the time), along with any number of the following elements:

- The Bible is the literal Word of God, inspired by the Holy Spirit and conveyed to the biblical writers directly from God. In other words, the stories, events, and actions of the Bible are true in a literal way. They do not necessarily need interpretation. The result of this is a general belief or assumption that these events (narrative stories, etc.) actually happened. What this means, for example, is that Abraham and Sarah were real people who really lived and who really did the things Genesis suggests they did. In the gospels, Peter really did momentarily walk on water when Jesus called to him on the sea; and doubting Thomas, in John's gospel, really did say he would not believe unless he "put [his] finger in the mark of the nails and [his] hand in his side" (John 20:25).

- God is the God of supernatural theism, the Creator of all that is and the Father of Jesus Christ, who has qualities that are both divine and human. God is also unchangeable (or, static)—the same yesterday, today, and tomorrow—and is notably more kindly tempered in the New Testament than in the Old Testament. Many who believe in this way also believe God has a plan for our life and salvation. A derivative of this is that everything that happens in life is in accord with God's will (i.e., everything happens for a reason, already known by God).

• Jesus is the Son of God, born of the Virgin Mary. Sinless himself, he has come to save us from our sins. Jesus is also an amazing miracle worker, having walked on water, brought people back from the dead, given sight to the blind, and turned water into wine at a famous wedding. Jesus' life and ministry, leading to his death and resurrection, are preordained by God and are part of God's plan for human salvation.

• Believers need only profess Jesus Christ as Lord and Savior, be baptized into the body of Christ that is the church, seek to live a Christian life, and then, upon death, receive the personal salvation the church promises. This promise includes eternal life in heaven for *believers*, as contrasted to a life of damnation in hell for nonbelievers (those who have not confessed belief).

• Jesus is coming again, supposedly after the rapture. These are distinct events—the rapture being a deliverance of the believers, while the Second Coming (coming after the tribulation) involves a time of judgment and sorting out. Most conservative-evangelical Christians expect these events to take place.

You may want to add to this list any doctrinal and moral teachings of the Christian faith that have shaped your own, personal understanding through the years. As we move forward, some general assumptions that underlie this book:

• The Bible, God, and Jesus are *believable* if they are presented in a more contemporary and progressive way, which is what I am attempting to do in this book. Such a way reflects our more evolved and enlightened ideas about life and the world, consistent with advances in biblical research and the teachings of modern science. Another way of understanding these ideas would be in terms of adequacy. In other words, how adequate are these ideas in their ability to describe and explain our modern world?

- As believers and aspiring believers, we ought to be able to use our minds and think rationally about the substance of our faith. Put another way, we should not be too easily satisfied by simply repeating the faith claims of previous generations.

- In this same vein, as children of the Enlightenment, the teachings of modern science, history, anthropology, and philosophy do not need to be in contradiction with what we believe as modern-day Christians. An obvious example would be evolution. A person can believe in evolution theory and still have integrity as a person of Christian faith.

THE TARGET COMMUNITY: WHO IS THIS BOOK FOR?

Within a broadly conceived understanding of Christian faith, this book is for persons who are interested in and/or curious about the life of faith and/or the life of the Spirit. It is for persons who have an itchy curiosity about faith, mystery, and the meaning of life. The target community for this book are the following:

1. People who have grown up in the church or who have been in the church for some time but who, in recent times, increasingly find the message of the church—the way the Bible, God, and Jesus are presented—difficult to believe. These are disenchanted Christians.

   I run into people all the time, such as Harry and Janet, a couple in their midforties. They have been dedicated church people all of their lives. However, in recent years, through personal study and progressive adult education experiences, they have been influenced by new ways of thinking about God, Jesus, and the Bible. When their church continues to resist new ways of thinking about the Bible and new ways of understanding God and Jesus, they become discouraged, sometimes to the point of wondering if there is a place for them in the Christian church.

2. People active in the church who are more or less content yet always open to new growth, new teachings, and new ways of understanding the Christian faith.

In most churches there are often people like Robin who, no matter the status quo of their current church, are open to new ways of thinking about life, faith, and the church. Robin is content enough with her own church. Still, she is always excited and engaged when new opportunities for learning come along.

3. Persons new to the church who believe in God, want to believe in the Bible, and are curious about Jesus. They haven't made a decision yet about identifying themselves as Christians; still, they are certainly prospects.

    There are always people coming into our churches who, although they do not know much about God, Jesus, and the Bible, are eager to jump in and learn. James and Kathleen were like this. In their early thirties and with two young children, they were open to whatever the church had to offer. They had a lot of questions. At the same time, they were motivated and eager to get started.

4. The intellectually and spiritually curious: people who are open to new ideas about the deeper questions of God, life, and the Spirit.

    There are always people in the community who have an itchy spirit for learning and growth. They may or may not consider themselves Christians, but they are notably intellectually curious and spiritually hungry. I remember Andrew being like that. I don't think he ever joined the church, but he liked to think about and be challenged by what he believed and about things spiritual in his life journey.

5. The unchurched: persons who have never gone to church or shown much interest in church. They are prospects if a progressive message about the Bible, God, and Jesus should ever meet their ears. Who knows how they might respond?

    These unchurched are anywhere and everywhere. Who knows what the reasons are that they have never darkened the doorway of a church. Still, if they could be invited to a church function and eventually have a chance to hear the church's progressive presentation of God, Jesus, and the Bible, a vibrant nerve might be struck and, down the road, they might find themselves checking out the church.

The Bible You Didn't Know You Could Believe In was written for all of these people and more, some of whom are members of my wider personal family. The purpose of the book is to offer an understanding of the Bible, God, and Jesus that while being faithful to the origins of our Christian faith is, at the same time, *believable*.

What I offer in this book is not necessarily new, although it might be new to some. The reflections shared emerge from forty-plus years of local church ministry, from a lifetime of wrestling with scriptures on sermon preparation, leading Bible studies, and, in general, thinking reflectively on the Christian faith.

THE PROBLEM

Traditional Christian teaching about the Bible, God, and Jesus isn't necessarily a problem until people, as they mature (sometime after middle school), start using their minds and begin to probe more deeply into the meanings and truth of faith claims they had always taken for granted. When this happens, the coherence of things often (gradually) begins to crumble and eventually much of what they learned in church and in the home (and believed over the years) begins to lose believability.

Over time, the consequence of this is increasing numbers of people leaving the church and turning away from the faith. For this group of people, the Christian faith that has been presented to them lacks the credibility to sustain their active commitment and belief. It is probably the case that many of these persons want to believe but simply find too many stumbling blocks. More and more, as they have matured, the faith of their childhood lacks believability. The way the Christian story continues to be presented is simply not adequate to their modern spirit and a more evolved way of thinking about life and the world. Large numbers of these same people would say they believe in God but have problems with the Bible. Many, too, are not sure what to do with Jesus.

In trying to understand this, recent surveys conducted by the Pew Research Center, which conducts research on religion and public life, says: "The number of Americans who do not identify with any religion [known as the *nones*] continues to grow at a rapid pace. One-fifth of the U.S. public—and a third of adults under 30—are religiously unaffiliated today, the highest percentages ever in Pew Research Center polling."[1]

Indeed, this is both the context and the challenge of our modern situation. The question for us is, how are we going to respond? We will turn now to a consideration of how we read the Bible.

---

[1] "Nones on the Rise," Pew Research Center Religion & Public Life, October 9, 2012, www.pew forum.org/2012/10/09/nones-on-the-rise.

CHAPTER 1

THE IMPORTANCE OF *HOW* WE READ THE BIBLE

We live more deeply than we can think. We think more than we can express.
—Bernard M. Loomer
("Process Thought and Religious Language," November, 1974)

All persons enjoy flashes of insight beyond meanings already stabilized in etymology and grammar.
—Alfred North Whitehead
(The Adventure of Ideas, page 227, 1933)

How we read the Bible is important. Our conceptual framework, the assumptions we make, the understanding we have about language—all of this is important and influences how we read and understand the biblical word.

When the Bible is freed from the oppressive constraints of biblical literalism, it becomes free to breathe, inspire, instruct, and enlighten us with the timeless truth, wisdom, and meaning that spring forth from its pages.

As we consider the importance of *how* we approach the Bible, some preliminary words on what language means and how it is used.

Language is humankind's imperfect effort to describe our experience. It is the only tool we have to relate our experiences, to unpack our deepest thinking, feelings, emotions, and intuitions. Our language can be beautiful and captivating to where it lifts our spirits and warms our hearts. Still, even in its most exalted and precise form, it is abstract. By abstract, I mean it is limited; it is partial and incomplete. For this reason, our language can only be *truth telling* to a point.

For us humans to acknowledge the inherent limitation of our language is a humbling experience. It reminds us that our words are at best only imitations of the deeper truths our minds and spirits seek to convey.

As my seminary professor Bernard M. Loomer has pointed out (*Process Thought and Religious Language,* November, 1974): "We live more deeply than we think, *and* we think more than we can express."[1] In other words, no matter how hard we try, our thoughts can never totally capture the depths and rhythms of our lives. And no matter the intelligence and the energy we put into our language, it can never live up to the depths and reaches of our thinking, feelings, and intuition.

As we consider the limitations of biblical literalism (or any literalism), this insight is helpful. It helps us understand even more the challenge of the biblical writers. Imagine, for example, that you are the author (or one of the authors, for we can seldom be certain about the number of authors) of the Gospel of Mark or the Gospel of John.

Mark was written sometime around 70 CE (common era), almost forty years after the death of Jesus. Whoever the author of Mark was, he probably did *not* know Jesus in the flesh. Therefore he probably received information about Jesus from any number of others.

A gospel is a telling of good news. In our Christian story, it is the *good news* of Jesus Christ (more on this later). However, for our present purposes, imagine the complexity involved in writing a gospel. To the best of your ability, you are seeking to write down some accounting, some remembering of Jesus of Nazareth. To begin with, imagine the challenge in gathering information about

---

[1] Bernard M. Loomer, "Process Thought and Religious Language," Nov., 1974.

Jesus—his teachings; his parables; his alleged miracles; the witnesses about him; his healings; his interactions with the disciples, others in the community, and the religious leaders within Judaism.

The gathering of this information is, at best, second- or thirdhand. In this sense, it is *history remembered*. It is the memory of someone (no doubt many some-ones) about all the different activities, interactions, and dimensions of Jesus' life. And bear in mind that whatever information (*remembered* experiences) is passed on, the actual event that happened (i.e., the teaching or the action of Jesus) is itself interpreted by the person who experienced it.

In other words, there are levels of abstraction (*abstraction* here suggests partial truth) right from the start. The author himself has to sort out the remembering and relate it the best he can, all within his own set of interpretive bias.

The larger point is that language is generally more complex than we tend to think. This doesn't mean that what Mark conveys is not truthful. It simply means that it is in no way *literally* truthful. It is at best an interpretive account of someone else's memories; it is history remembered and history metapho-rized (history captured, as best it can be, in metaphorical narrative).

And consider the Gospel of John. John was probably written toward the end of the first century, around 100 CE. Most scholars think John had between three and five authors. Imagine the challenge of the final editor. It is likely that at least some of these authors were members of what we call the Johannine commu-nity, or the community out of which the Gospel of John and the three letters of John emerged.

In John's case, some seventy years have passed since Jesus died on the cross. Seventy years in antiquity is a long time. Imagine the mutations, additions, and deletions that have taken place in the Gospel of Jesus that the authors of John seek to put into words. It may well be for this reason that most progres-sive biblical scholars believe there is little in John that actually happened in an historical sense. Virtually all of John, therefore, is memory conveyed through metaphor and symbolic language. It is *post-Easter* metaphorical narrative on evolving understandings and experiences of Jesus.

Again, the fact that it is metaphorical narrative doesn't mean it is not true. In fact, I would argue that the Gospel of John, precisely because it is mostly symbolic language (i.e., metaphor, story, and creative discourse), is the most truthful of the four gospels. More on this in the section ahead on metaphor and symbolic language.

Again, a pillar assumption of this book is that the Bible was not written to be taken literally. It is not inerrant, nor is it infallible. In fact, to read the Bible in a literal way is to miss out on much of the Bible's creative possibilities to impart truth and inspire and expand faith.

To reiterate, *how* we read the Bible is important. It should be pointed out that the rise of fundamentalism, which is fueled by biblical literalism, is a relatively recent development (late nineteenth to early twentieth centuries). The problem is that during the twentieth century, and now into the second decade of the twenty-first century, popular Christianity in our culture continues to be articulated in ways that suggest an underlying literal reading of the Bible.

In cases where people are perhaps less persuaded by a literal reading of the scriptures (i.e., in many mainline Protestant denominations), much of the language and assumptions underlying their beliefs are tinged with the general theology (and Christology) of biblical literalism. It has simply become the religious language in our wider American culture and life. It is the language we use. We see this in the birth narratives from Matthew and Luke at Christmastime; and again at Easter in the gospel stories of Jesus' crucifixion and resurrection.

We will reflect on all of this in different ways in the pages ahead when we discuss more deeply the believability of the Bible, God, and Jesus. In discussing *how* we read the Bible, the underlying thesis of this book is that the Bible should be read:

- in light of its historical context
- to a great extent, as metaphorical narrative and symbolic language

These two elements are critical to a more enlightened understanding of the Bible. The use of *enlightened* here suggests an understanding that allows for evolution of thought and new understandings flowing from modern scholarship and learning. *Enlightened* means letting new light into the way we see and experience the Bible, the life of faith, and the world.

HISTORICAL CONTEXT

The Bible is an account of God's relationship with a particular group of people (Israel), written over a period of more than eleven hundred years (approximately 980 BCE to 125 CE). Think about that! In its entirety, the Bible was written in retrospect, or after the fact. Much of the Bible was edited (rewritten) and then—some of it—edited again.

The gospels of Jesus, our overwhelming primary source for information and learning about Jesus, were written some forty (Mark) to perhaps seventy (John) years after Jesus died. Spend a few moments contemplating the mutations any memories or witnesses of Jesus most likely went through. As memories of actual events are passed on over time—through an oral tradition—some degree of change (by addition or subtraction) is bound to occur.

Also, it is important to bear in mind that every biblical writer had some agenda, some purpose in mind. For example, each of the gospels emerged out of a particular, concrete community of believers. Within these communities there were certain strengths and weaknesses (as in any community of believers), certain problems the writer was attempting to deal with in whatever way. In other words, the books of the Bible have a context, a real-life situation out of which they emerged. For bible study to be adequate to our experience, for it to be relevant and meaningful, historical context must be taken seriously.

Still, thinking about context, we can only know so much. While it is important to know what we can about what happened in a historical sense (i.e., Did this really happen?), nonetheless, it is a contention of this book that questions of *meaning* are more important than questions of a historical fact. In other words, rather than "Did this really happen?" it is more helpful to ask, "What does this mean?"

METAPHOR AND *SYMBOLIC LANGUAGE*

To read the Bible responsibly, it is important to understand that the Bible was never intended to be a history book or a book on science or any other academic discipline. While the Bible does contain accounts of events that historically probably happened, much of the Bible is, more accurately, history remembered and then interpreted. Oftentimes the memory is two, three, or more persons removed. Put another way, it is not helpful to think of the Bible as history in the normal sense. Indeed, it is useful to view the Bible less as actual history and more as spiritual story.

But if the Bible is not actual history, then what does this suggest about the truth of the Bible? Is the Bible true? My response is a profound *yes*, but not in a literal sense. Again, in understanding the Bible in the big picture of things, it is important to remember that what the Bible means is more important than whether something actually happened. In other words, the Bible *is* true, but it is true with regard to its larger meanings. Put another way, the spirit of the Bible (its essence) is true; the values and meanings the Bible conveys are true.

Many of the teachings and meanings of the Bible come to us through stories, parables, and poetry. In this context, much of the language of the scriptures is metaphorical, or symbolic language.

For example, do we think the youthful David, generally considered Israel's greatest king, actually killed a giant named Goliath in a real confrontation? Very improbable. However, that doesn't mean that the teaching of the story is not truthful—that faithfulness to God (David) cannot overcome great odds (taking on Goliath). David is lifted up as being faithful, courageous, and re-sourceful. Because of his faithfulness, Israel is victorious over the Philistines. In this instance, those who appear to be needy and vulnerable are, in fact, strong and powerful when buoyed by faith. Indeed, in faith all things are possible.

Again, the point to be made is that much, if not most, of the Bible is memory metaphorized, or memory related through symbolic language (whether these biblical accounts actually occurred is not as important as the meanings that are transmitted). As memories of events, actions, and teachings are passed on from person to person through the years, the language used to capture these experiences is increasingly metaphorical or symbolic.

When I say most of the Bible is written in symbolic language, this is merely to assert that it is *not* recorded history as we generally understand it. Let us say it again: the Bible is *not* history, nor is it science, philosophy, psychology, or any other academic discipline. The Bible is the story of God's relationship with a particular group of people (Israel) over a period of approximately two-thousand years (from the nineteenth century BCE with Abraham and Sarah, to the early second century CE with the letter of 2 Peter). To say this even more compellingly, it is a story—related mostly through metaphorical narrative (symbolic language)—of the formation and life of our Judeo-Christian heritage.

By symbolic language, I mean language that is not describing direct, actual experience but rather indirect experience that has been passed on. Using symbolic language, the author seeks to tell his story in ways that are persuasive, given his particular goals and purposes. To make his point, he may tell a story, recount a tale or parable, or use any number of rhetorical devices to relate the larger truth he wishes to convey.

Consider the richly symbolic story of the wise men in Matthew's birth narrative. The story begins with the star in the east and the brilliance of its light that will guide the alleged wise men to Jesus' birth at Bethlehem. No doubt this light is a reminder of the light referred to in Isaiah 60 where the author, Third Isaiah (Isaiah 56–66), says:

> *Arise, shine; for your light has come, and the glory of the LORD has risen upon you. For darkness shall cover the earth, and thick darkness the peoples; but the LORD will arise upon you, and his glory will appear over you. Nations shall come to your light, and kings to the brightness of your dawn.* (Isaiah 60:1–3)

For Matthew and the faith community out of which his gospel emerged, the meaning of Jesus' life and teachings is so profound that, indeed, "nations shall come to [his] light, and kings to the brightness of [his] dawn." For them, the *Christ event* has universal meaning symbolized by the Gentile wise men following the heavenly light. This is all beautifully created metaphorical narrative revealing the universal message of God's love. The larger point is not the literal truth of anything the gospel writers seek to communicate but rather the deeper truth, teaching, or meaning they seek to share. Again, take the patriarchs and matriarchs: Abraham and Sarah, Isaac and Rebekah, and Jacob and Rachel. We don't have incontrovertible proof that they actually existed, nor do we know any actual facts of their lives. We do know, to some extent, what a particular tradition says about them and what their lives and stories mean for the larger story of Genesis.

When we think of the importance of metaphor, story, and parable in the Bible, my guess is many people are quick to debunk metaphor as somehow inferior to factuality. No doubt, this grows out of our tendency to think of metaphor as *not real* or less real than some actual fact or firsthand recording of an event. If our larger purpose is truth, however, metaphor has much to offer and would certainly not be thought of as inferior.

In his book *The Heart of Christianity*, Marcus J. Borg recalls that German novelist Thomas Mann once defined myth (an expression of metaphorical narrative) as "a story about the way things never were, but always are."[2] With this in mind, is a myth true? Understood in this light, it is not literally true, but it is really true.

In this same vein, a priest once noted in a sermon, "The Bible is true, and some of it actually happened." A similar point was made by a Native American storyteller as he was reflecting on his tribe's view of creation: "Now I do not know if it happened this way or not, but I know this story is true."

When Jesus says in John's gospel, "I am the light of the world" (8:12); or, "I am the bread of life" (6:35), or "I am the good shepherd" (10:11), the terms *light, bread of life,* and *good shepherd* are metaphors that point to deeper meanings and truths. While they are not literally true (i.e., Jesus is not actual light), they are in a sense more truthful than true. In this sense, metaphor is symbolic

---

[2]Thomas Mann, in Marcus J. Borg, *The Heart of Christianity: Rediscovering a Life of Faith* (San Francisco: HarperOne, 2003), 50.

language. Symbols point to larger realities, to larger truths. They suggest meanings that are expansive and go beneath the surface, meanings that embrace feelings, intuition, mystery, and a sense of wonder.

DISTINCTION BETWEEN PROSE AND POETRY

In our emphasis on the use of metaphor in the Bible, I want to comment on the difference between the language of prose and poetry. Keep in mind that while most of the Bible is prose, still, much of the Bible is poetry (e.g., the Psalms and much of the prophets). Prose is typical language; it is straightforward, commonplace, and generally flat. It has its place, but it falls short of poetry in important ways.

Poetry is the language of the heart and spirit. It is language that is lofty, rhythmical, creative, imaginative. Poetry elevates our thoughts as it warms our hearts. Poetry gets at the world of human feelings, emotions, intuitions, and mystery. The poet has an enviable capacity to inspire and to move us to deep feelings and meanings.

When speaking of truth, our feelings are the most concrete (i.e., truthful) expressions we have of our human experience. They are deeper and more truthful than words. More than the writer of prose, the poet seeks to embrace and explore these feelings and put them into words. In this sense, there is a truth to poetry that transcends the truth of prose. It is helpful for us to bear this in mind as we encounter the scriptures.

OUR CONCEPTUAL FRAMEWORK: IDEAS AND MEANINGS

An important element in *how* we read the Bible has to do with the conceptual framework that each of us brings to our life experience. As we encounter the world, day after day, what ideas and values inform our experience? Through what ideas and values do we see relationships and experience events? How do these ideas and values guide us and shape us as we live our way through life?

Books about the Bible, God, and Jesus are inevitably books about ideas and meanings. These ideas and meanings have to do with the underlying principles and beliefs about what we believe and why we believe as we do. Our thinking on important matters rests, in part, on these principles. They help shape the motivation behind the way we respond to our life experiences.

Our primary ideas about reality—about life and the larger world in which we live out our lives—are important. These ideas are the lenses through which we view the world. They help us understand and make sense of our everyday experience. More still, they guide us in the ways we think about God (theology) and Jesus (Christology), as well as the ways we interpret the Bible.

In my life, I have been deeply influenced by the ideas of process/relational modes of thought, garnered largely from the teachings and person of Bernard M. Loomer, again, a professor of mine in seminary at the Graduate Theological Union in Berkeley, California. For me, Loomer became not only an enlightened mentor but also a dear friend.

Professor Loomer always emphasized five foundational ideas/principles that describe reality. It should be noted that these principles (he called them *elephantine* principles) are not the end-all of cosmological reflection and truth. But they are, for the moment, a place to start. As a minister and a writer of sermons and articles (twice-monthly articles over thirteen years for a local newspaper), Professor Loomer has been a tremendous help to me through the years.

Again, these five ideas/principles are understood to be (for me, at this time) the most adequate ideas for understanding the universe that I know. Very simply, the ideas are:

Process. The truth of the world is that life is in process. Along with the universe, our lives are constantly unfolding and evolving. They are in process; they are decidedly not static. This is also true for God, relationships, communities, and situations, along with our personal and collective histories. They are forever in process, forever unfolding and becoming.

Relationality. Life is relational. Indeed, individuals are literally formed and shaped by their relations. Our relationships define who we are. We become human beings in relationship to other human beings and to God. In this sense, we are fundamentally relational and social creatures. A relational view of life has significant meanings with regard to how we view the world. Consider power, for example. A relational view of power suggests that as individuals, we both influence and are influenced by the other or others. We do not simply influence another person, in a unilateral sense, without being influenced ourselves. The life of any social group (family, team, club, work situation, council) is relational. There is back-and-forth, ongoing interaction, learning and growing taking place all the time.

Relativity. The truth of life is relative; it is relative to the particular experience of every form of life. Every person has a perspective relative to his or her own experience and life journey. The relativity of our present life situation says volumes about who we are in any given moment. The saying, "we cannot really know a person unless we walk for a time in their shoes" would apply here. The reaches of relativity are seen in response to the question: In a church of one hundred people, how many theologies are there, and how many approaches to reading the Bible? The answer is there are one hundred of each because each person's theology or way of reading the Bible is relative to his or her own life experience.

Ambiguity. Life is ambiguous, which means the truth of our life experience has multiple meanings. For example, our greatest strength as a person is often the source of our greatest weakness and vulnerability. The ambiguity of life opens the slippery door of complexity in life. Life is complicated. Ambiguous meanings and nuances of understanding abound in the grip of the ongoing chaos, confusion, contradiction, and mystery of our shared lives. A sensitivity to ambiguity enables us to venture beneath the surface of common experience to uncover truth and meaning that might otherwise be left unexplored.

Tentativity. The truth of life (and of the world) is also tentative, which means it is not necessarily forever. For example, how we feel or think today is not necessarily the way we are going to feel or think tomorrow, or next week, or next year. The tentativity of life reminds us of the importance of not making premature conclusions, not making too much of the moment. In other words, the moment (who we are today) does not capture the totality of who we are as an evolving person, which is always changing. We are always in the process of becoming something more.

To repeat, these ideas need to be understood in terms of adequacy as opposed to perfection criteria. How adequate are they (not, How perfect are they) in helping us understand the truth of our common human experience in the present? As you let the vibrations of these ideas settle in, you will readily note how they sometimes overlap and interrelate.

As we consider these ideas and their meanings, it is important to remember that they are a response to the question, What is it that is truthful about reality, about the world and the universe? What is descriptive about life in the most expansive and general sense? In this regard, it must also be stated that the ideas that inform the way we view and understand the world ought to be able to be applied as well to our understanding of God, Jesus, and the Bible. Put another way, the best ideas about what is truthful about reality (about the universe) ought to be truthful as well about God, Jesus, and the Bible.

To illustrate, the idea of process, cited above, asserts that the world (the universe) is in a constant process of becoming. The world is not static; it is in process. The idea of process has significant implications when applied to God, Jesus, and the Bible. With respect to God, for example, God is not static or *not* not evolving and *not* not growing. Rather, God is always in the process of unfolding, of evolving, even to the point of transcending God's self. The God I refer to is *not* the God of supernatural theism; God is not an actual being hovering over the world, somehow orchestrating events here on earth. Rather, God is Spirit; God is infinite energy, love, and mystery. God is everywhere and anywhere, all at the same time.

Seeing God in this dynamic way opens all sorts of doors to the way we understand God and relate to God. The always evolving God is more alive and interesting than a God that is simply always the same, never changing. Through the eyes of process, God is more creative, more inviting, and more open to relationship. Seeing God in this light helps us appreciate that God, too, is a feeling spirit. God is not unaffected by or unfeeling about the suffering in the world. God, too, grieves and mourns the sadness and tragedy of our human situation.

In another example of the importance of process, the recent Supreme Court decision in support of same-sex marriage reveals the ideas that helped shape Justice Anthony Kennedy's summing up of the court's five-four decision. He pointed out how the Constitution is always more than a totally static and settled document (i.e., it is part of an evolving process). It remains responsive to the evolving opinions and experiences of the American people. As our opinions as a nation have evolved over the years, our understanding of the Constitution has evolved at the same time.

Adding to this, the relational (*relationality*) and relative (*relativity*) meaning of the Constitution has evolved as well. There is perhaps nothing in our culture that captures the depths of relationality quite like marriage. Marriage offers us humans the deepest, most intimate and sacred union of our love and affection. To have the right to marry rejected by the state would be to exclude same-sex couples from this high and sacred union. It would serve as well to diminish them as human beings, along with their attendant families.

As a living document, the Constitution must be interpreted relative to the unique and particular experiences and values of the American people. The relative context with regard to same-sex marriage has changed in recent times. Justice Kennedy's perspective (along with the other four justices) affirms this change and thus renders an interpretation that is responsive to the relativities of our evolving world.

The point I am trying to emphasize is the importance of looking at life and the world through the lenses of our most truthful (most adequate) ideas about life and the world.

CHAPTER 2

THE PROBLEM WITH BIBLICAL LITERALISM

My point, once again, is not that those ancient people told literal stories and we are now smart enough to take them symbolically, but that they told them symbolically and we are now dumb enough to take them literally.

—John Dominic Crossan, on Literalism

The problems with biblical literalism are numerous. To begin with, when we start to work our way through the Bible, we soon become aware that it is flawed at numerous points. Falsehoods, inconsistencies, and contradictions are commonplace.

At the outset, there are two, somewhat contradictory creation stories in the Hebrew Scriptures: one in Genesis 1:1–2:3 and the other in Genesis 2:4b–3:24. The first story is most likely a more recent version than the second. Also, there are three versions of the Ten Commandments: Exodus 20, Exodus 34, and Deuteronomy 5. None of this is necessarily a problem in terms of the meaning that is conveyed. However, when the Bible is claimed to be infallible and inerrant, it creates obvious problems. What are we to believe?

In a more serious vein, however, as we work our way through the Torah (the first five books of the Hebrew Scriptures), some of the actions credited to biblical figures and to God would be considered wrong, immoral, and even evil by almost any standard. In the face of these behaviors, as reasonable people of faith, how can we continue to argue for biblical inerrancy and infallibility?

In Exodus 15, for example, God is presented as rejoicing in the drowning of the Egyptians at the Red Sea. Was this God not also the God of the Egyptians? In this same book of Exodus, slaves could be mercilessly beaten by their masters, and children who cursed or struck their parents could be executed (Exodus 21). These and other parts of the Torah suggest severe punishment—even death—for all sorts of behaviors and actions.

In parts of the Hebrew Scriptures, God is promoted as a tribal God. Tribalism is typically fraught with excesses in loyalty and the tendency to lift one's tribe above any other group. Children of the Edomites, for example, had their heads dashed against rocks (Psalm 137:7-9); the Midianites were ordered destroyed (Numbers 31:1-2); Midianite children and females who were not virgins were to be killed. Meanwhile, Moses allowed the Israelite men to keep the virgins for themselves. Problems of tribalism abound in the Hebrew Scriptures.

As we consider the Christian Scriptures, we need to first point out that while these scriptures were written in Greek, Jesus spoke in Aramaic. Yet the scriptures contain almost no words of Jesus speaking Aramaic. (*Talitha Cumi*, from Mark 5:41, and *Eloi Eloi lama sabathani*, from Mark 7:34, would be exceptions.)

Also, as it turns out, the idea of the virgin birth has no solid basis in scripture. Neither the word *virgin* nor the notion of virginity are found in the Hebrew text of Isaiah that Matthew quoted to support his account of Jesus' virgin birth. The understanding of *virgin* is present only in the Greek word *parthenos*, used to translate the Hebrew word *almah* in a Greek version of the Hebrew Scriptures.

In the gospels, sometimes the gospel writers put strong words in Jesus' mouth that would seem to be contrary to anything he might say. "Brood of vipers" (Matthew 12:34), says Jesus of his enemies, and "blind fools" (Matthew 23:17). Earlier, Matthew has Jesus refer to the Gentiles as "dogs" (15:26). In Matthew 12:46-50, Jesus supposedly disowns his family.

John's gospel is noted for very suggestive language regarding the Jews. These references, which are numerous, have a pejorative ring to them. More, still, is

John's suggestion that the Jews "loved darkness more than light because their deeds were evil" (John 3:19). And the implication in John 8:39–44 is that the Jews were children of the devil.

From this short list of references we can see the problems involved in thinking the scriptures are infallibly inspired from God. What kind of a God would act in this way?

As we reflect on the gravity of these problems with the Bible, we have to ask ourselves, Why weren't more of these elements of the Bible edited out during the significant editing that took place during the Exile and at other points in Israel's history?

As we can easily begin to see, the problem with biblical literalism is that the more you learn about the Bible, about when and how it was written, and about the considerable number of inconsistencies, errors, and contradictions that fills its pages, a literal reading of the Bible makes less and less sense. Worse yet, it suggests a view of God (and Jesus, too, to a lesser extent) that is both objectionable and unbelievable.

The influence of biblical literalism on Christians and aspiring Christians has had a larger negative impact than is generally realized. My sense is that most people, both in and out of the church, are not aware of this. Most people naturally assume certain things about the Christian faith without much probing.

Notions about God and Jesus are routinely shared in American culture, and many of these notions are limited and do not suggest a God or a Jesus of much size or stature. The reason for this, more than people realize, is that the language and faith about God and Jesus have been largely shaped by a literal reading of the scriptures that has simply been passed on from generation to generation.

INITIAL REFLECTIONS ON GOD

At this juncture I want to note some possible stumbling blocks for faith suggested in the New Testament when we read the scriptures literally. However, before I do this, I want to make some initial comments on God.

To begin with, God is always *more* than our efforts to explain and understand God. The God I refer to in this book is a God of spirit, of energy, and of infinite mystery and love. It is *not* the God of supernatural theism. The God of supernatural theism is *out there*, above and beyond, generally detached and distinct from life here on planet earth. Within traditional Christianity, this is the God people think of and pray to when they refer to God. The God of supernatural theism (generally considered to be an actual being) is a God who is all-powerful and all-knowing. This is the God who intervenes when God chooses in our human and communal lives and also in creation.

Again, the God I present in this book (similar to the God of panentheism, where God is both immanent and transcendent) is a God of spirit, infinite energy, love, and endless mystery. God is also infinitely compassionate and just. God is anywhere and everywhere at the same time. Once again, God is always *more* than anything we might say about God. For example, God is coextensive with the unfolding of the universe—and more. God is relational, comprising all God's relationships to all forms of life—and more. God's abiding passion is LIFE (and more), which is why God, metaphorically, called the world into being and breathed life into Adam at the dawning of creation.

God is not an actual being out there somewhere, external to life here on earth. Rather, God is spirit that is anywhere and everywhere (again, at the same time). As spirit, energy, love, and mystery, God works through relationships—through us as human beings and communities, and also through the ongoing process of the unfolding of creation. It is not God's nature to interfere in the freedom of humans to choose, nor in the freedom of the universe to self-create. More on all of this in the chapter on God.

STUMBLING BLOCKS FOR FAITH

There are a number of traditional Christian teachings that, if taken literally, become stumbling blocks for faith. By *stumbling block* I mean a teaching about God and/or Jesus that, upon serious thought and reflection, does not make sense and serves to make the Christian faith less believable. Over time, stumbling blocks can lead people to turn from the church and the life of faith. I already noted the discrepancies with the idea of the virgin birth, which is retold every year in Christmas pageants around the world.

Does God Have a Plan for Our Lives?

The idea that God has a plan for our lives has always troubled me. Proponents of the God-has-a-plan idea point to a whole range of verses, in both the Hebrew and Christian Scriptures, which they cleverly interpret to support this contention. In my many conversations with people, this seems to be a fairly common belief. Indeed, it can be a comforting thought. However, a major problem exists: it is bad theology.

A corollary to this belief is: everything happens for a reason (supposedly because it is a part of God's plan). People tend to think like this, as if nothing happens in life that is outside of God's plan and purpose. Again, bad theology.

Without mentioning human responsibility and freedom, what about when things go badly for us in life? What about when we are the victim of seemingly random violence, a debilitating injury, or losing our house to foreclosure? Are we to think these sudden (often random) misfortunes are a part of God's plan for our lives? This sort of thinking paints a picture of a notably capricious and unkind God, a God of dubious character, a God of limited compassion and love.

Consider infant mortality, for example, or the death of any loved one! In every instance, is this a part of God's plan? Or an airline disaster where two-hundred-plus persons are killed—was that a part of God's plan? Were they supposed to die in this way? Or persons who are suddenly confronted with a life-threatening illness and in two months they are dead. Was this a part of God's plan? When the mother of three young children is tragically killed in an automobile accident, was it, too, a part of God's plan?

If these sorts of human experiences are part of God's plan, do we not have to ask ourselves, "What kind of a God is this?" This is certainly not a God I could believe in. The God I know does not will tragedy on anyone. The God I know is a God of infinite love, compassion, unending forgiveness, and passion for justice. The God whose holy name I call on is a God of tenderness and grace that never run out.

For me, to think of God in this way invites unbelief, not belief. I could not believe in this kind of a God. Think how many people are turned away from the church and the Christian faith all the time because they think this understanding of God is the God they are supposed to believe in. To reiterate, this is bad theology. It is a very reduced way of thinking about God. More on this in chapter 4, "Believing in God."

Before mentioning some additional stumbling blocks to faith, it is important that we make a distinction between the pre-Easter and post-Easter Jesus, which I will discuss later in chapter 5, "The Jesus You Didn't Know You Could Believe In." At this point, we need to remember that most of the gospel stories are metaphorical narratives on the post-Easter Jesus, again written forty to seventy years after his death and resurrection.

Did Jesus Die for Our Sins?

In the church, we have been told forever that Jesus died for our sins. In the Pauline epistles, it is cited again and again. Indeed, it is one of the core traditional teachings of our Christian faith. If read metaphorically, as an expression of the radical grace of God, it captures the way the early church thought about the role of Jesus in their faith journey. The problem is, for us moderns, if taken literally, as it is in conservative-evangelical Christianity, it doesn't make sense. Worse still, it paints a picture of God as severe, even cruel.

The idea of Jesus dying for our sins grew out of the Temple theology within first-century Judaism. At the time, the Temple had a monopoly on the access to atonement sacrifices for an array of sins. If Jesus were viewed as the sacrifice for sin (as having died for our sins), this would help support the Pauline notion that the advent of Christ, and him crucified, signaled an end to dependence on the law.

I do not believe Jesus died for our sins, nor do I believe the pre-Easter Jesus thought his death would in any way be linked to saving people from their sins. I believe he died out of faithfulness to God, put to death by the sins of the world (the convergence of Roman law and Jewish Torah). I cannot conceive of Jesus waking up one day and saying, "I think I'll go get crucified for the sins of the world." It makes no sense. From God's point of view, how could a loving God will such horrific suffering on any human being? (More on this in the chapter on Jesus.) If the crucifixion were God's will, what would that say about God's character and nature? More still, would such a God be a God we could believe in?

With all of this in mind, its needs to be said that, consistent with God's nature, God always does what God can to bring good out of evil, light out of darkness, and life out of death. This is who God is; it is what God does. Part of the meaning of the resurrection is, indeed, God's vindication of Jesus in the face of the evil of worldly powers. In the resurrection, which probably took place over a period of months, if not years, God's energy of love and impulse for life win the day.

The Second Coming of Jesus

Another stumbling block is the biblical assurance of the Second Coming of Jesus. Approximately one-third of American Christians believe literally in the Second Coming. They have heard it read from the scriptures and preached on in services of worship; they hear other Christians make reference to it in Bible studies. No doubt, they and others think it is something Christians are supposed to believe. With this in mind, even though a literal belief in the Second Coming would seem to defy belief, what are they to do?

I do not believe in the actual, literal Second Coming of Jesus. However, if we look back to the post-Easter communities evolving after Jesus' resurrection, we can understand how believers would want to preserve a vital sense of Jesus being present to them—and in as tangible a way as possible.

Also, some years later, after the destruction of Jerusalem and the Temple by the Roman empire around the year 70 CE, apocalyptic eschatology (suggesting the end of the world) became an increasingly plausible belief for many. Indeed, within Judaism there had been an expectation that the resurrection of the Messiah would lead to some final end-of-time event in history.

However, for me, a compelling idea in support of the Second Coming (understood metaphorically) is that it originated in the context of a social hope. It wasn't meant to be taken literally. No doubt, it evolved over time. We have to remember that the period between Jesus' death and the first New Testament writings (Paul's letters) marked some twenty years. Given the suffering and plight of the peasant class (who comprised the overwhelming majority of Jesus' followers), the Second Coming as social hope would have a lot of appeal.

Interestingly, the earlier writers of the New Testament (i.e., Paul and, later, Mark) were the ones with the most to say about the Second Coming. In the later gospels, Luke and John, it is not directly mentioned (nor is it mentioned in Romans, one of Paul's later letters). Again, the return of Jesus very likely evolved over the years as a means of giving hope to people locked into circumstances of human suffering. It gave the least of these hope for a better tomorrow; the intent was never that it be taken literally.

I should note that, with respect to the Gospel of John, a recent book by John Shelby Spong, *The Fourth Gospel: Tales of a Jewish Mystic*, makes the argument that the Second Coming ("coming" of the Spirit) was indeed Jesus' breathing on the disciples in the third resurrection narrative of John (John 20:21–22).[1] In this narrative, Jesus comes to stand among them. After showing the disciples his hands and his side, he says to them:

> "Peace be with you. As the Father has sent me, so I send you."
> When he had said this, he breathed on them and said to them,
> "Receive the Holy Spirit. If you forgive the sins of any, they are
> forgiven them; if you retain the sins of any, they are retained."
>
> (John 20:21–23)

---

[1] John Shelby Spong, *The Fourth Gospel: Tales of a Jewish Mystic* (HarperOne, 2013), 295–296.

For Spong, this breathing on the disciples was indeed a *breathing on* of new life and new consciousness that Jesus came to bring. Spong adds that, in the ancient creation story of the Hebrew people, God had initiated a "first coming" of the Spirit when God breathed the breath of life into Adam.

The Miracles, or "Mighty Deeds," of Jesus

A further stumbling block of faith are the miracles, or "mighty deeds," of Jesus that appear throughout the gospel stories. They are rich, poetic stories of hope, healing, and empowerment. Jesus turning water into wine at the wedding in Cana; giving sight to the blind; healing the lame; calling Lazarus out of the tomb of death to life; walking on water to call the disciples to greater faith. Jesus heals paralytics, cleanses lepers, raises a widow's son, feeds "the five thousand" people on five loaves and two fish, and restores sanity to a demoniac.

People are amazed, and their amazement inspires faith and lifts the spirit. Clearly these miracle stories—*mighty deeds*—have their place. They convey truth in the larger sense; but most of them are not true in a literal sense (although Jesus may have actually done some healings). However, walking on water, turning water into wine, feeding the five thousand (with two fish and five loaves), restoring sight to the man born blind, and raising Lazarus to life—it is unlikely that Jesus actually did these things.

What Jesus did was love with deep compassion and kindness. Indeed, these qualities exuded from his spirit. He spent time with people, listening to them, teaching them, healing them, seeking to surround them with his spirit and presence. More still, he challenged the authorities on their behalf—on behalf of the poor, the sick, the distressed, the marginalized, the victims of whatever injustice or unfairness.

What people knew was that when Jesus was with them, they felt the presence of the Spirit; they felt more alive, more full of hope, more reassured about the future. There was something life-changing about Jesus' way and about his teachings and the *God presence* that was in him. (It should be noted that most Christians are unaware that there is nothing in the New Testament about Jesus as a miracle worker until the eighth decade CE.)

With this in mind, after his death and resurrection, as the years passed (close to forty years between his death and the earliest gospel), stories about Jesus glowed with deeds of power and teachings of wisdom. When the gospel writers began to write about him, they wrote in lofty language that sought to convey the way people had remembered him and felt about him.

This was not unusual for the ancient world. In other words, the miracles that were attributed to Jesus, more than anything, were testimonies of his love and compassion, his mercy, understanding, and grace. They were testimonies of the ways God's power and Spirit were alive in him. People felt about him in ways that led them to write about him in this way.

Rather than feeling pressure to believe things about Jesus that defy belief, seeing Jesus' mighty deeds in this way inspires faith. To see the size of Jesus' love and spirit shine through the lofty metaphor of the gospel writers feeds our faith and invites in us even greater belief.

Still, to flat-out reject the miracle stories because, read literally, they lack believability is to miss out on the larger truth the miracles point to. The miracles are important not because we should believe they actually happened but because of what they say to us about Jesus and what they mean to us about the possibilities for faith.

TAKING THE BIBLE SERIOUSLY BUT NOT LITERALLY

We are seeing how the limitations of biblical literalism, even when they are subtle, spill over into the way we think about what the Bible says. And if what the Bible literally says causes unbelief in people, it becomes a problem. Over time, it keeps people from embracing the Christian faith and from attending our churches.

That is why it is important to illustrate the limitations and consequent problems posed by a literal reading of the scriptures. In this vein, we can see how taking the Bible seriously requires that we not take it literally. Such a reading of the Bible simply doesn't make sense.

Indeed, the only way biblical literalism can be defended is on the loose grounds that at every stage of writing, interpreting, and editing, it was divinely inspired by the Holy Spirit. In this manner, it came directly from God. This, of course, involves a major stretch of the imagination.

No matter the length of time between the actual historical event and the date the biblical writing occurred; no matter the number of times the story or event was passed on in the oral tradition from person to person; no matter that it was edited, and perhaps edited again and again; no matter that numerous events and behaviors in the Bible, when taken literally, stand against any common standards of love, compassion, forgiveness, and generosity of spirit; a literal reading of the Bible defies logic and reason. At some point, over time, people begin to notice this. When they do, understandably, they have questions about believability. But again, those questions arise in a context that has been influenced over decades and decades by language growing out of culturally ingrained assumptions that the Bible was the literal Word of God.

The Bible should be read and understood from a big picture perspective, from the vantage point of the whole. We must never too simply reduce the Bible to one verse or one chapter, or even one book. The Bible is always more than any of these reductions. For the Bible to breathe freely and continue to inspire, it must be liberated from the burden and the flaws of inerrancy and literalism.

As a humbling perspective on the scriptures and also as context, we need to remember that the Bible was written over a period of eleven hundred years. I continue to be amazed at this disclosure. Eleven hundred years (from approximately 980 BCE to 125 CE)! There were countless authors along the way, most of whom remain anonymous, and lots of editing and reediting as well.

Again, the thesis of this book is that if we do not take the Bible literally but rather read the Bible (1) in light of its historical context and (2) as metaphorical narrative and symbolic language, the Bible is abundantly believable. Both God and Jesus are understood in more believable ways as well.

It should be noted that the biblical writers did not intend for the Bible to be read in a literal manner. They had no awareness of the more modern notion of the inerrant Word of God. They wrote with the literary tools and ways of their particular historical period. Much of what these writers wrote came to them through the oral traditions of the times. Often the truths they spoke of were woven around the Babylonian and Mesopotamian myths and legends that were popularized in their culture.

A literal reading of the Bible leaves out so much. By treating biblical stories and events as if they really happened in a factual way, never looking beneath the surface, we miss out on the larger message related through the symbolic language used to describe the stories and events. In terms of stature, a literal reading of the Bible is small. It has limited size. It is unable to nudge us to a larger world. It doesn't challenge the mind and spirit with questions and curiosity that can take us to deeper meanings and truths.

Take the Gospel of John, for example. Virtually all of the stories (e.g., the wedding at Cana, Nicodemus, the Samaritan woman at the well, etc.) are metaphorical narratives, not actual historical happenings. The larger purpose of these stories (and, indeed, of John's gospel) is to convey spiritual meanings and insight, not descriptions of historical events. The resurrection stories are other examples of this, as we will see in the chapter on Jesus.

MISUSING THE BIBLE

Another problem growing out of a literal interpretation of the Bible is the way the scriptures can easily be used as an instrument of control, like a club or a hammer. Pastors and others who claim too easily to know the Bible (*the Word,* as they like to call it) can be more than a little proud and arrogant in the way they talk with people about the Bible.

Oftentimes, new Christians and others can feel put down by the way pastors and Bible study leaders refer to the Bible with such certainty of perspective and conviction. It is as if there were no wiggle room for questions and doubts to be expressed. Sadly, biblical literalism can be too easily reduced to rigid and simplistic doctrine where reason and wonder have no place.

Finally, a literal reading of the Bible is flat and closed. Lacking imagination and creativity, it keeps us from a deeper experience of God. Moreover, it lacks a full appreciation of context. Because of this, it lacks the possibility of taking us to higher spiritual ground and to a deepening and enlarging of the internal relationships in our family, community life, and beyond.

TRUTH AND HISTORICAL CONTEXT

Truth and meaning in the Bible have everything to do with context. That is why the idea of context is so important in the way we read the Bible. To make the point again, the Bible should always be read in light of its historical context. To abstract any scripture verses out of their context has the potential to significantly distort the larger truth and meaning that was intended.

Selectively abstracting verses in this way, often to support our own biases and prejudices, can readily become a tool of control and manipulation. Pastors, church leaders, and others can too easily use the Bible in this short-sighted way to support virtually any point they want to make.

For example, if we take the Bible out of context, Paul's views on the role of women can become problematic. In both Ephesians and Colossians, Paul (or teachings attributed to Paul, emerging out of the Pauline school) says:

> Wives, be subject to your husbands as you are to the LORD. For the husband is the head of the wife just as Christ is the head of the church. . . . Just as the church is subject to Christ, so also wives ought to be, in everything, to their husbands. (Ephesians 5:22–24)

In general, in New Testament times, women were expected to assume subordinate roles in the family, community, and corporate worship. However, in modern times, for us to read first-century attitudes on the role of women into the second decade of the twenty-first century would be more than a little presumptuous and short-sighted, and would make us unpopular with more than half the human family. Attitudes on women have significantly evolved over the centuries, as well they should have, just as attitudes and thinking on race and homosexuality have evolved as well.

In modern times, Paul has taken a lot of criticism for his first-century words on the role of women—sometimes, I believe, unfairly. In fact, in his time, Paul was a relative progressive on women. In Paul's first-century world, women were typically viewed not only as totally subservient to their husbands but also as third-class citizens or worse. Paul exhorts men to love their wives, even to love their wives as they love themselves (Ephesians 5:33). Again, for his time, Paul's view of women was relatively progressive.

The larger point is that the scriptures have a historical context that should be honored in the process of our reading and interpretation. Reading the Bible contextually challenges us to ask: What is the larger truth the biblical writer is seeking to convey? And, how is that truth applicable to us in our modern life-situation?

Because gays and lesbians have suffered so extensively over the years, a contextual reading of the biblical passages used to demonize them is perhaps even more important. For example, Leviticus 18:22 is often used to support biblical condemnation of homosexuality. However, in this same larger section of scripture, Leviticus also says, "you shall not sow your fields with two kinds of seed; nor shall you put on a garment made of two different materials" (Leviticus 19:19). Just as these two prohibitions seem ridiculous to our modern minds, they also caution us not to make too much of other prohibitions Leviticus makes.

As we reflect on controversial questions such as gender role, homosexuality, and racism, we have to remind ourselves that historically, the Bible has been used again and again to support personal bias. It is therefore helpful to ask ourselves two questions: (1) What does the best of the Bible say to us about how we respond to controversy? (2) How might God want us to respond?

Clearly, the best of the Bible, particularly as it is reflected through the life and teachings of Jesus, would want us to respond out of a spirit of love, compassion, forgiveness, justice, mercy, and generosity. Typically these are the quintessential Christian virtues.

As for God, in the Bible God is overwhelmingly about life:

- A wind from God sweeps over the face of the waters and the world is created.

- God breathes life into the spirit of Adam and Eve and humankind springs forth.

- Through Moses, God sends commandment truth with the primary goal to preserve life. (Indeed, the Ten Commandments are mostly about sustaining the life God has given us.)

- Over the years, prophets are sent forth to preserve the covenants (life-sustaining accords).

- In the Christian scriptures, God calls us to life through the person of Jesus.

Whatever God's will is, its most basic impulse is a passion for life. God's concern about any idea, claim, behavior, or action is, Is it life-giving? Does it give life to the community and to the world? Put another way, does it enlarge the stature and spirit of the other person or the community?

Along with this, our modern context for reading the Bible needs to consider that attitudes on matters such as gender role, racism, and sexual orientation are always in a process of evolving. To read the Bible with love and compassion in our hearts today is to take seriously how these very attitudes have changed and evolved. To do otherwise is to render us irrelevant to our unfolding community and world.

The Hebrew Scriptures

To think that the Bible was authored over an eleven-hundred-year period boggles the mind. And who knows the number of authors involved, to say nothing of the origins of all of the accounts, stories, and memories? With this in mind, to suggest that these biblical writings, with all the complexity that surrounds them, should be read in a literal fashion, as if they were somehow free from any imperfection, is more than a little incredulous.

The compilation of the Hebrew Scriptures had to have been an arduous task. Four different traditions—the Yahwist (around 980 BCE), the Elohist (about

850 BCE), the Deuteronomist (620 BCE), and the Priestly (after 597 BCE)—all coming from distinct historical periods and situations, and each writing from a unique and particular perspective.

The Yahwist was writing from Jerusalem with his slant on the history of Israel. The Elowist wrote from Samaria, the capital in the north, with his version of this history. Later, the tradition of the Deuteronomist emerged, based on a scroll reportedly discovered during repairs to the Temple in the reign of King Josiah. The book was known as *deutero*, or the second giving of the Law. It was a book stressing the kind of reforms emphasized by the prophets. Still later, the Priestly tradition arose in response to the Exile of Israel to Babylon (587–538 BCE). A very complicated historical period, the priestly writers edited and re-edited much of the traditions that had been passed on to them.

As we can see, the version of the Hebrew Scriptures that emerges is one interpretation after another of history remembered and revised. There were often good reasons for the revisionist editing. But still, to suggest that these scriptures are even close to being literally true would stagger the imagination.

Again, we must ask ourselves, what is the larger truth being conveyed? The Deuteronomist, for example, would certainly be concerned with justice and concern for the poor and the marginalized (thus, many of the teachings in Deuteronomy). Meanwhile, the priestly tradition was confronted with the very deep and complicated realities of the Exile. Israel had lost everything. The monarchy, along with the religious elites and the aristocracy, had been deported. The Temple had been destroyed, along with Jerusalem, and the Torah had been carried off. How was Israel to understand this? This was beyond tragic. It was cataclysmic. What would the priestly editors say about this?

This was the period of the great prophet of the Exile known as Second Isaiah (550–539 BCE). He was the poetic author of the well-known suffering servant chapter, Isaiah 53 (Isaiah 40–55 is the prophetic activity of Second Isaiah). Later, New Testament writers would seek to explain Jesus' own suffering on the cross by looking back into history to the suffering servant in this gripping poetry.

The Christian Scriptures

As we consider the Christian Scriptures (50–125 CE), aside from Paul, virtually all of the authors were anonymous. Paul is generally credited with writing seven of the letters attributed to him (Romans, 1 and 2 Corinthians, Galatians, Philippians, 1 Thessalonians, and Philemon). The other letters—Ephesians, Colossians, 2 Thessalonians, 1 and 2 Timothy, Titus, and Hebrews—identified with Paul were most likely (with the probable exception of Hebrews) penned by members of the Pauline school (disciples of Paul).

With these Pauline letters, along with the other letters in the New Testament canon, the historical context alluded to above is of utmost importance. Each letter was written with regard to a particular community or setting with its own particular set of problems. Each author had a particular goal and purpose in mind when he sat down to write. Although we can never grasp the full measure of the historical context, it is important that we give it our best effort.

The gospel stories were very complex undertakings. Think of the challenges involved! First, how to choose the author; or maybe they were not chosen but simply set out on their own. Whatever the case, one day the author of Mark's gospel sat down and began to write.

Who knows exactly what sources he had before him? He had his own sources, to be sure. And as scholars suggest, he also probably had what is known as Q, which stands for *quelle*, or "source" in German. Q comprises mostly sayings attributed to Jesus. Beyond this, the author had his own personal story, along with his own biases and opinions (this would be unavoidable).

Very likely he was a member of some evolving Christian community as well, with all its particular challenges and issues. Keeping all of this in mind, writing a gospel would be a process that is both personal and communal. Still, forty to seventy years after Jesus died, it would be farfetched to suggest that these gospel accounts were all somehow inerrant and literally true.

THE BIBLE AS BELIEVABLE AND INSPIRATIONAL

The good news in all of this for Christians and seekers (persons seeking to be Christians), and certainly for the church, is that when we move beyond the huge problem that biblical literalism poses for the Christian faith, we are left with a faith that is not only believable and relevant for our modern experience but also inspirational and deeply meaningful.

For me, part of what makes the Bible so believable is that it is such a profoundly human document. If we think about it, can we begin to imagine the amount of human effort—the long hours of tireless labor that hundreds and, more likely, thousands of human beings put into the formation of the Bible? It boggles my mind when I reflect on the complexities involved in putting together what we call the biblical canon. And, of course, there were many apocryphal books that did not make it into the sixty-six-book canon.

Legions of human beings over the centuries gave themselves to the task of writing, editing, reediting, and translating these holy scriptures. When we think how these stories—some of them ancient and others of them still more ancient—were passed on and on over the eons of time, we are humbled and grateful. When we think how the story of the Ten Commandments evolved over the years and all that was involved in its telling and retelling; when we think of the parables of Jesus and where they might have come from, and the impact they have had on the story of Jesus; when we think of the timeless wisdom of his teaching over the centuries, we are humbled and awed.

When I think back on all of this, when I allow myself to begin to absorb all that is involved in the story of the Bible, I am inspired. It is a deeply inspirational story. The more we discover how human the Bible is, the more impressive it is. The Bible is a living testimony of how we human beings have searched and yearned for God. It is a testimony of how we have been humbled by God, forgiven by God, and renewed by God. The Bible knows how we humans have ached to the depths of our humanity to know even a glimpse of God's presence. The Bible knows. And because the Bible knows, we cannot help but be inspired and called to life:

I was silent and still; I held my peace to no avail; my distress grew worse, my heart became hot within me. While I mused, the fire burned; then I spoke with my tongue: "LORD, let me know my end, and what is the measure of my days; let me know how fleeting my life is." (Psalm 39:2–4)

The Bible knows!

For my thoughts are not your thoughts, nor are your ways my ways. . . . For as the heavens are higher than the earth, so are my ways higher than your ways and my thoughts than your thoughts. (Isaiah 55:8–9)

The Bible knows! God knows! And together they inspire.

CHAPTER 3

THE BIBLE YOU DIDN'T KNOW YOU COULD BELIEVE IN

Once we free the Bible from the burden of biblical literalism, the stories of the Bible begin to take on a new life in our minds and spirits. Suddenly the wedding at Cana and the raising of Lazarus take on new meaning. Soon, as well, the stories of Jesus' crucifixion and resurrection are seen in new and expanded light. If we stay with it and give the spirit a chance to move in our lives, the Bible can be an enormous source of new meaning and purpose.

As we reflect on the believability of the Bible, I want to make some general affirmations about the scriptures that can be helpful to us along the way. Taken as an aggregate, all of these affirmations work together in helping us see the Bible not only as more believable but also as eminently deserving of the respect and honor we have given it over the centuries.

THE BIBLE IS A HUMAN CREATION

The Bible is a human product and creation. It was not written by God. God is spirit, energy, infinite love, and endless mystery. God doesn't write things. While I do believe God was a source of tremendous inspiration to the biblical writers (and editors), I do not believe God authored the Bible. Again, human beings wrote the Bible.

Theologically it is important that the God of our faith is a God who is consistent from one generation to another, from one century to another. In our modern era, it is not in God's nature to write things. This is not something God does. Therefore, to be consistent, if God does not write things in our century, it makes no sense to believe God wrote things in some previous century. Again, God did not write the Bible. God is not the author of the metaphorical narratives, stories, teachings, parables, and poetry of the Bible.

It needs to be said that the Bible is in no way diminished because it is of human origin. Indeed, if we think about it, the fact that the Bible was written by human beings is a tremendous accomplishment. It is humankind's effort to relate the best stories we know, along with the deepest understandings and meanings these stories have given us over the centuries, to future generations. That is a profound achievement.

Also, there is the matter of human responsibility for the biblical canon (the Bible as we know it). Human beings made the choices about which books (narratives, prophecies, gospels, letters, etc.) were included in the canon and which were left out. Unavoidably, there was some level of arbitrariness to this decision-making process. This is another instance of the Bible not being an inerrant and infallible document. Moreover, as a human creation, it continues to invite our human interpretation and response. In this sense, the Bible as canon is always open-ended. It is always open to new and fresh insight and understanding.

THE AUTHORITY OF THE BIBLE

Because the Bible is of human origin, the authority of the Bible is not God. The authority of the Bible—the power and impetus that have enabled the Bible to survive all these years—is rooted in the relationships of individuals and communities of faith who have continued to tell and retell the biblical stories over the centuries. Of course, their relationship to God is of vital importance. In their own time and own way, these communities of faith (both Jewish and Christian) continued to hear the voice of the Bible and bear witness to the claim it has on their lives. This claim is the foundation of the Bible's authority.

I cannot stress too strongly how important it is (to say nothing of being remarkable and impressive) to observe that the Bible has survived so well all these years. In this sense, the Bible has paid its dues. In other words, it deserves to have its stories told. Over centuries, each generation has had to sort out the meaning of the Bible for itself. The authority of the Bible continues to rise up from communities of faith as they tell and retell the biblical stories over the passing decades.

THE BIBLE AS MYSTERY AND WONDER

Part of what makes the Bible so believable is that, when we break away from literalism and give it a chance to breathe, it nudges us beyond ourselves. It invites us to embrace the world of mystery and wonder. The mystery of God, along with the mysteries of love and life, are always inviting to the human spirit. They are a refreshing reminder that our lives are always on some trajectory of change and transformation. Our lives are not static. Our faith is not totally settled. God and the Spirit are always beckoning.

Mystery and wonder point to that great beyond that forever looms. A new sense of possibility. A first-time feeling about love, or some special spiritual awareness or connection. New meanings and consciousness are born in these unique experiences.

Think of God calling Moses to go to Pharaoh in Egypt and "bring my people, the Israelites, out of Egypt" (Exodus 3:10). When Moses protests, thinking he is not qualified, God persists. Finally, Moses says to God:

> If I come to the Israelites and say to them, "The God of your ancestors has sent me to you," and they ask me, "What is his name?" what shall I say to them? God said to Moses: "I AM WHO I AM." He said further, "Thus you shall say to the Israelites, I AM has sent me to you." (Exodus 3:13–14)

To this day, our best biblical scholars cannot be certain what this reference to I AM means. Does it refer to God as totally *other*, as ineffable and impenetrable? Does it speak of God's radical freedom to be who God is but not in a way we can grasp? Mystery and wonder overflow in this phrase about the I AM that is our God.

And consider the closing verses of 1 Corinthians 12 that lead into Paul's famous love chapter, 1 Corinthians 13. After enumerating the different gifts of the spirit, Paul says, "But strive for the greater gifts. And I will show you a still more excellent way" (1 Corinthians 12:31).

Then the beautiful and evocative words of 1 Corinthians 13 fill the air: "If I speak in the tongues of mortals and of angels, but do not have love...." Coming the to last five verses before the final verse, we read:

> *Love never ends. But as for prophecies, they will come to an end; as for tongues, they will cease; as for knowledge, it will come to an end. For we know only in part, and we prophesy only in part; but when the complete comes, the partial will come to an end.*
>
> *When I was a child, I spoke like a child, I thought like a child, I reasoned like a child; when I became an adult, I put an end to childish ways. For now we see in a mirror dimly, but then we will see face to face. Now I know only in part; then I will know fully, even as I have been fully known.* (1 Corinthians 13:8–12)

Then the chapter concludes: "And now faith, hope, and love abide, these three; and the greatest of these is love" (1 Corinthians 13:13).

These verses radiate mystery and wonder. Where else in Western civilization can you find such beautiful and penetrating poetry? We are all on this progressive journey called life. The *now* of life we know only partially, but one day the complete will come and the partial will come to an end.

And later, "For now we see in a mirror dimly, but then we will see face to face. Now I know only in part; then I will know fully, even as I have been fully known" (1 Corinthians 13:12).

About all I can say to this is *WOW!* Indeed, the Bible invites us in; through mystery and wonder it invites us in. And through the mystery we are reassured. For God knows us. One day we will know what we cannot know on this side. And it is all good; for we ourselves have been fully known.

THE BIBLE AS SACRED AND SACRAMENTAL

The sacred is anything that is of God; it is something worthy of our veneration and reverence. The sacramental is something that mediates an experience of God or of the Spirit. The Bible is sacramental when the language of its stories, narratives, and poetry evokes in us an experience of God or the Spirit. Such experiences of God and the Spirit happen fairly often in Bible studies and in personal meditations on the scriptures.

Take, for example, Psalm 139. The sacramental possibilities of this psalm would seem to be limitless. Consider the power of this psalm to mediate an experience of God or the Spirit:

> *O LORD, you have searched me and known me. You know when I sit down and when I rise up; you discern my thoughts from far away. You search out my path and my lying down, and are acquainted with all my ways. Even before a word is on my tongue, O LORD, you know it completely.* (Psalm 139:1–4)

And later:

> *Where can I go from your spirit? Or where can I flee from your presence? If I ascend to heaven, you are there; if I make my bed in Sheol, you are there. If I take the wings of the morning and settle at the farthest limits of the sea, even there your hand shall lead me, and your right hand shall hold me fast.* (Psalm 139:7–10)

The presence of God coupled with the infinite mystery of life's ways draws us in. Taken metaphorically, the words of the psalmist are reassuring. There is an expansive sense that we are known and understood by one greater than we. There is the sense as well that God (or the Spirit) is with us; that we are not alone. These words overflow with sacramental impulse and feeling. We feel the warmth of God's presence and spirit.

Also, consider the Beatitudes, the first eleven verses of Matthew 5 from Jesus' Sermon on the Mount. The sacramental impulse of these verses is both gripping and powerful:

> *Blessed are the poor in spirit, for theirs is the kingdom of heaven.*
> *Blessed are those who mourn, for they shall be comforted.*
> *Blessed are the meek, for they shall inherit the earth.*
> *Blessed are those who hunger and thirst for righteousness, for they will*
>   *be filled.*
> *Blessed are the merciful, for they will receive mercy.*
> *Blessed are the pure in heart, for they will see God.*
> *Blessed are the peacemakers, for they will be called children of God.*
>
> (Matthew 5:3–9)

What immediately grabs us about these situations of blessedness is their humanity. Each of these states is a state of vulnerability, a human state or condition that yearns for more of God, more of the Spirit. The sacramental energy of these words evokes in us an immediate response of love, compassion, and intense feeling. We feel the closeness of God and the Spirit.

The Beatitudes are infused with the power of the sacred and suffering love. Again, we can feel it. It is a feeling beyond words, a feeling that points to the holy. And as the meaning of these beatitudes begins to fill our spirits, it takes us to higher spiritual ground.

The Bible is sacred because its stories have become over time the best stories we know. Let us move to highlight some of these best stories as, together, they not only point out the Bible's believability but also the important role the Bible has played over the years in our individual and communal lives as well.

THE BEST STORIES WE KNOW

To say the stories of the Bible are the best stories we know is a profound statement. Step back for a moment and think about this in light of the vast resources available to us for learning and acquired knowledge. "The best stories we know" is a riveting and powerful claim. It says a lot about our history and culture, both in and outside the church. Such a claim cannot be made lightly. It can only come after years and years—indeed, generations and centuries of experience.

Not only do these best stories affirm the believability of the Bible, but there is also a compelling sense in which the Bible, as the best stories we know, has a claim on our lives. As we reflect on all of this, indeed, what are some of these best stories?

The Creation Stories

The creation stories of the Bible are among the best-known stories in American culture, and no doubt in Western civilization and beyond. Virtually everyone has heard of them. Not everyone is aware, however, that there are two stories (Genesis 1:1–2:3; and Genesis 2:4b–3:24). In terms of chronology, the second story (known as J, for the Yahwist) is actually the earlier version and probably dates to the tenth century BCE; the first story (known as P, for *priestly*, the familiar six-days-of-creation story, with God resting on the seventh day) was almost for sure written during or after the Exile (587–538 BCE), most likely in the 500s BCE.

The creation stories are myths, which does not mean they are not true; only that they are not literally true. Although the idea of myth is typically debunked in our culture, dismissed as being false and something notably less than a scientific explanation of things, myths have a truthfulness of their own that deserves our respect and listening ear.

For the world of religion in antiquity, myth sought to make a connection between the supernatural and creation as people experienced it. Myth is purely metaphorical, using symbolic language to offer explanations of things. In the ancient world, myth was humankind's best effort to make sense of reality.

Think for a moment about the enormous challenge at hand! If you were attempting to describe the origin and nature of the universe, what would you say and how would you say it? Not an easy question. In our modern world, we take so much for granted because of the tremendous advances in modern science. But if you were writing some three thousand years ago, how would you go about it? Beyond what the science of the day could teach you, all you know are the reigning mythological stories of your day. So you do the best you can to connect the dots in your perceptual world: the earth, the seas, the sun, the moon, the stars and the heavens, animal and plant life of all forms, and, of course, human beings, along with your sense of the human situation.

A critical part of the creation story surrounds the serpent and the temptation in the Garden of Eden. God has already told Adam and Eve *not* to partake of the forbidden fruit from the tree of the knowledge of good and evil. As we know, they both yield to the serpent's tempting, whereupon they are forever banned from the garden (to a life east of Eden): Adam to a life of endless tilling of the soil and Eve to an existence of greater pain in childbearing.

Genesis does not refer to this succumbing to temptation as the Fall, or as the birthplace of original sin (i.e., suggesting we are born into sin). Rather, it is a metaphorical glimpse of the human situation. Clearly something went wrong. As human beings, we start out in paradise, yet after failing the test with the serpent, we are banished to lives of exile and anxiety. How are we to understand this? Indeed, what went wrong?

The traditional Christian response is that sin is born in us, that we are sinners from birth. As tradition would have it, our salvation from sin comes through Jesus Christ, who died for our sins on the cross. If we confess our belief in Jesus as Lord and Savior and have faith that God used his death to save us from our sins, our salvation is secure and, upon our death, heaven awaits us. There are all kinds of problems with this traditional understanding, which I will deal with in detail in chapter 5, "The Jesus You Didn't Know You Could Believe In."

However, when we read the creation stories as metaphorical narrative, another response emerges of what went wrong (my personal view), illuminating the fullness of the human situation. Endemic to our humanity is an inborn desire to know more than we can know and to want more than we should want. We humans do not have an easy sense of our human limits. Put another way (and more strongly), there is something in us that wants to be God, that wants all knowledge and all control. We want to be in charge of our destiny.

The birth of this desire—our propensity for sin or to be more than we can be—builds up within us as our consciousness evolves, as we become increasingly aware that we are mortal, that we are *not* God. This raised consciousness leads to a life "east of Eden" and to a life of relative and unending anxiety. It is the human situation.

The balm for this anxiety is humility and love. But we have to work at it. We are never totally free of the anxiety. Another way of understanding this state is that we are never in control of our lives. Always there comes a point where we have to trust. We have to trust the love, forgiveness, and hope as we live gracefully unto death and into the ultimate mystery of God.

Why Two Creation Stories?

In noting the two different creation stories, we might ask, "Why the two stories?" Again, historical context is so important. The second creation story—written during the Babylonian Exile (587–538 BCE) but appearing first in Genesis (Genesis 1:1–2:3)—was most likely added by the priestly editors (known, again, as the P tradition) to emphasize the importance of the Sabbath. In the story, God creates the world in six days, but on the seventh day God rests:

> *So God blessed the seventh day and hallowed it, because on it God rested from all the work that he had done in creation.* (Genesis 2:3)

In the Exodus version of the Ten Commandments (also, most likely edited by P during the Exile), great emphasis is again placed on the Sabbath:

Remember the Sabbath day, and keep it holy. Six days you shall labor and do all your work. But the seventh day is a Sabbath to the LORD your God. (Exodus 20:8–10a)

To repeat, the historical context for this later version of creation (appearing first in Genesis) is the Exile, the cataclysmic event marked by almost unimaginable destruction for Israel. Jerusalem, along with the Temple, was destroyed, razed to the ground. The king and royalty were deported along with the elites of every stripe (only the peasants were left behind). The Torah was carried off to who knows where.

This utter destruction understandably caused unspeakable turmoil along with desperate concern for Israel (now living in Babylonian exile). How is Israel to understand this destruction? In relation to God, what went wrong? How could this have happened? Was Israel not God's chosen people?

Clearly something went terribly wrong. Had Israel neglected the covenants? Had she accommodated herself too much to the domination system of the ruling elites, both political and religious? Over time, had she exploited and eventually forgotten the poor?

The priestly editors (the P tradition) edited a significant portion of the Hebrew Bible during the Exile, most likely in an attempt to respond to these grave concerns. Most importantly, in an effort to sustain Jewish identity in a foreign land, they sought to emphasize the central role of Sabbath observance by connecting it to God's creation at the beginning of time. Circumcision was also emphasized by these priestly writers. In trying to make sense of their experience of the Exile, these two observances together stressed the significance of covenantal obedience.

Very probably, these priestly editors had an additional motivation as well. Wanting to do everything they could to help Israel get right with God, they sought to be real clear about the importance of Sabbath observance and therefore incorporated it indelibly into their creation story.

The Exodus

The Exodus is *the* paradigmatic story in the Hebrew Bible. It is the pinnacle event in Israel's memory that, again and again, reminds her of who she is as a nation and as a religious people. Israel is *that* nation, *that* people, whom God rescued from exploitation and oppression at the hand of the iron-fisted Pharaoh in Egypt. The Exodus event has decisively revealed the character and will of God.

What does this mean? What this means is that the will of God always stands against the domination systems (another term for this would be *empire*) of the world. Typically, domination systems control people through economic exploitation and political oppression, often supported by religious legitimization. Indeed, the history of empire reflects this.

In Israel's history, empire includes Egypt, Assyria (during the destruction of the northern kingdom of Israel in 722 BCE), Babylon (during the destruction and deportation of the Exile, 587–538 BCE), Persia, Alexander the Great (i.e., Macedonia/Greece), and eventually Rome during the time of Jesus. To the point, it is the nature of empire to exploit, oppress, and, when applicable, seek to legitimize power in the name of the gods and religion.

Indeed, the story of God in the Bible (both Hebrew and Christian Scriptures) is the story of promise and fulfillment in the face of one domination system after another. Throughout the Bible, from Egypt to Rome, God's voice of promise and fulfillment is relentless. It cannot be held back. It is simply who God is and what God does.

The story of empire is the story of the human situation. It is what we humans tend to do when our spirit and ego are not transformed, when we do not heed the invitation of the spiritual high ground. (In metaphorical language, the spiritual high ground is that place where love, compassion, humility, and unwavering hope fill the air. It is holy and more—a high ground beyond words, with meaning and feeling; washed in love). For people of faith (and people of the Spirit), the spiritual high ground always beckons.

The Bible is believable because its stories, when not read literally, tell the truth about our human situation. The Bible's truth telling and expansive insight into human nature and the divine-human relationship are profound. When we let the Bible breathe (by not burdening it with a literal reading), it can draw us into its immense wisdom and help us make sense of the deepest meanings and feelings of our human experience.

Summing up, the Exodus is Israel's primal narrative. It is *the* quintessential story that tells Israel, again and again, who she is as a nation and a people. Israel is *the* people that God rescued from the oppressive hand of Pharaoh and the domination system in Egypt. The Exodus is a decisive liberation story of God's character and will.

The Ten Commandments

When people think of the Judeo-Christian ethic or world, almost immediately they think of the Ten Commandments. These commandments hold a sacred esteem within both Jewish and Christian culture and communities of faith. While the historical origin of the Ten Commandments is very likely rooted in Egyptian religion or in different law codes in the Near East of antiquity, still, these commandment truths have achieved a status all their own.

While tradition claims that Moses received these commandments from God on tablets of stone at the holy mountain (Mount Sinai) before entering the promised land (the culmination of the Exodus story), the story of the Ten Commandments should be read as metaphorical narrative. The story is true, but it is not literally true.

At the outset, we hear these words:

> *Then God spoke all these words: I am the LORD your God, who brought you out of the land of Egypt, out of the house of slavery; you shall have no other gods before me.* (Exodus 20:1–3)

Right away, the primal story in the Hebrew Bible, the Exodus experience, is announced as context for the commandments. Reference to this primal event in both Jewish and Christian faith signals that something important is about to be said. "You shall have no other gods before me" sets the stage for the nine commandments that follow. These commandment truths are touchstones of guidance about who we are and what our lives are to be about. In other words, we are the people for whom these commandments hold immense qualitative meaning. "Adhere to these commandments," God is saying, "and you will live."

A word about the Ten Commandments and God's purposes. In the big picture of the Bible, God is about Life with a capital *L*. In the "in the beginning" account in Genesis 1, in six consecutive pronouncements, God calls the world to Life ("Let there be light," and so forth). Later, in Genesis 2:7, God breathes "the breath of Life" into Adam (Eve comes later, from a rib of Adam). The covenants to which God calls Israel are about sustaining the Life of the community. The Ten Commandments, too, are about Life.

For example, violation of commandment introduces a distorting element into community life. When we dishonor our parents or ignore the Sabbath, our lives become disjointed. When we steal, kill, lie, commit adultery, or covet, a disruptive and chaotic element enters our relationships. Our lives become out of balance. All of these abuses of commandment work against the Life to which God calls us.

I point this out to reinforce the larger point that *the Bible knows*. The stories of the Bible, coming to us through God's relationship with us over the centuries, overflow with wisdom, truth, and meaning. In the trenches of our human adventure, God has been there. The beauty of this divine-human relationship is that Life marches on. Into the mystery and wonder that tomorrow will bring, God calls us to Life, and we move into the future with hope and promise.

The Prophets

In reflecting on the believability of the Bible, the biblical prophets, along with their proclamations, teachings, and insights, are probably the most instantly believable. I say this because the prophets would not exist were it not for the reality of human sin. If we were a sinless people, the prophets would be out of work; they would have to find a new vocation.

As we look at the prophets, it is helpful to divide them into three general groups:

1. The earlier, *cultural* prophets (Moses, Samuel, Nathan, Elijah, and Elisha)

2. During the period of the monarchy, the *classical* prophets, representing *the prophet as social critic* (Amos, Micah, Jeremiah, and Ezekiel)

3. During and after the utter despair of the Exile in Babylon, the *prophet as energizer of hope* (Second and Third Isaiah—Isaiah 40–55 and 56–66, respectively)

Since the time of Moses (thirteenth century BCE), prophets were always a part of Israel's cultural and religious life. From early on, the prophet was understood to be a spokesperson for God. These cultural prophets, as I refer to them, were not necessarily forecasters of doom or hope, like the more classical prophets. Yet they were part of Israel's community life and were available on a sort of as-needed basis.

For example, after King David, in a mood of passion, made Bathsheba (the wife of Uriah the Hittite) pregnant, he schemes to have Uriah killed in battle. Displeased with David's sinful actions, God sends the prophet Nathan to David with an indicting parable of good versus evil (2 Samuel 12:1–7). Not realizing that the prophet's parable was really about his sinful actions, David's anger kindles to where he cries out, "As the Lord lives, the man who has done this deserves to die" (2 Samuel 12:5). Whereupon Nathan says to David, "You are the man!" (2 Samuel 12:7).

The prophets of Israel, particularly the classical prophets, were amazing human beings. They had to be. They were men of immense courage and conviction. Again, they had to be. Whatever the historical context, the prophet was always a spokesperson for God. Imagine for a moment the burden (to say nothing of the responsibility) of this role in community life—the tension of speaking truth to power, for example, for an Amos or a Jeremiah.

What king would want to wake up to read this in the morning newspaper:

Woe to those who lie upon beds of ivory, who lounge on their couches, and eat lambs from the flock, and calves from the stall; who sing idle songs to the sound of the harp, and like David improvise on instruments of music; who drink wine from bowls, and anoint themselves with the finest oils, but are not grieved over the ruin of Joseph. Therefore they shall now be the first to go into exile, and the revelry of those loungers shall pass away. (Amos 6:4–7)

Then Amos goes on indicting the behavior of the elites of Israel, announcing the doom and destruction that is already at hand:

Hear this, you that trample on the needy, and bring to ruin the poor of the land.... The LORD has sworn by the pride of Jacob: Surely I will never forget any of their deeds. (Amos 8:4,7)

Amos is prophesying to the northern kingdom of Israel (capital at Samaria), which will eventually be destroyed by the Assyrians in 722 BCE. Some 120 years later, Jeremiah speaks a similar message of judgment to the southern kingdom of Judah (capital at Jerusalem). Jeremiah is but a young man (early twenties, perhaps). Imagine the antipathy and wrath his words inspired in the elites of his day:

Will you steal, murder, commit adultery, swear falsely, make offerings to Baal, and go after other gods that you have not known, and then come and stand before me in this house, which is called by my name, and say, "We are safe!"—only to go on doing all these abominations? Has this house, which is called by my name, become a den of robbers in your sight? You know, I too am watching, says the LORD. (Jeremiah 7:9–11)

Perhaps no prophet suffered the public scorn of his people as did Jeremiah. The rulers of his day wanted to put him to death (they finally chose a more muted response). Amos, too, suffered public vilification and rebuke. Imagine what their home life and life in community must have been like! Where could they go? With whom could they interact? Suffice it to say, the prophet as social critic had a tough life.

Eventually, from 597 to 587 BCE, the southern kingdom of Judah was destroyed by the Babylonians and all but the peasants of Israel were deported off to almost fifty years of exile in Babylon, a defeat and humiliation from which Israel never fully recovered.

The pinnacle prophetic voice as an energizer of hope was Second Isaiah (Isaiah 40–55), the poetic voice that rose up in Babylonian Exile with riveting words of hope and promise for a new day. In order to grasp the power of the prophet's poetic utterance, again, context is everything. Second Isaiah's period of prophetic activity was toward the end of Israel's almost-fifty years of exile in Babylon. Israel had lost everything in the devastation (Babylon put Jerusalem under siege from 597 to 587 BCE). The experience of the Exile was overwhelmingly the lowest point in Israel's history.

Hear the prophet's words:

> A voice cries out: "In the wilderness prepare the way of the LORD, make straight in the desert a highway for our God. Every valley shall be lifted up, and every mountain and hill be made low . . . then the glory of the LORD shall be revealed, and all people shall see it together, for the mouth of the LORD has spoken." (Isaiah 40:3–5)

"The way of the LORD" and the "highway for our God" refer to Israel's return home from exile. These are powerful words of hope for a new day, a word Israel desperately needs to hear, so profound has been her darkness and gloom.

Second Isaiah again:

> Do not fear, for I have redeemed you; I have called you by name, you are mine. When you pass through the waters, I will be with you; and through the rivers, they shall not overwhelm you; when you walk through fire you shall not be burned, and the flame shall not consume you. For I am the LORD your God, the Holy One of Israel, your Savior. (Isaiah 43:1b–3a)

And then later in the same chapter:

Do not remember the former things, or consider the things of old. I am about to do a new thing, now it springs forth, do you not perceive it? I will make a way in the wilderness and rivers in the desert. (Isaiah 43:18–19)

The "new thing," of course, will be the defeat of Babylon by the Persians in 538 BCE, after which Israel is free to return to her homeland. In fact, only a few thousand probably returned, and their return was, as one might imagine, a very difficult and rough-edged transition. Still, this motif of exile and return continued to serve as a powerful religious metaphor of our human situation.

The relationship of Israel's prophets to God and to their communities is a profoundly human story. These pillars of faith experienced the whole gamut of human experience: from virtually every imaginable trial and tribulation to the still faint hope of a new day. They tugged and wrestled with God and with themselves. Yet through it all, the flame of God's Spirit burned in them. They stood tall in relation to their calling and continue, through their timeless words, to invite us all into the mystery and wonder of God's presence and God's call to justice.

The Wisdom Teachings

Part of what makes the Bible such a rich and compelling document is that it includes this large section of scripture known as the wisdom literature, or the Writings. These writings include Job, the Psalms, Proverbs, Ecclesiastes, and Song of Solomon. But they have also come to include the book of Daniel, the books of Ruth and Esther, and the historical books of 1 and 2 Chronicles, Ezra, and Nehemiah.

An initial distinction of the wisdom writings is that they do not appear to correspond to any actual historical events. This makes the writings difficult to date with much precision.

Although the wisdom of the Bible is often connected to the personality of King Solomon (tenth century BCE), the wise king is not thought to be the author of any of the books. Indeed, the era of the wisdom teachings seems to be in the exilic (587–538 BCE) or post-exilic period, after 538 BCE.

Part of what I love about the wisdom teachings (and what makes them so utterly believable) is how very human they are. Indeed, they are often considered a little *too* real for some of our more conservative-evangelical brothers and sisters. Ecclesiastes, for example, is largely existential philosophy; and Song of Solomon is erotic love poetry. Neither of these literary genres is what normally comes to mind when people think of the Bible.

Yet it is precisely this kind of diversity that makes the Bible so relevant and meaningful (to say nothing of believable) in any generation. As we will see, the issues with which the wisdom writings deal are among the most core issues and questions of life for which there are no easy answers. We begin by looking at Psalms, which covers a vast range of human life and experience. We will then look briefly at Proverbs, and more extensively at Ecclesiastes, Song of Solomon, and Job. Through it all, it will become increasingly apparent how these writings are some of the best stories we know.

Psalms

What is immediately impressive with the psalms is how they touch on virtually every human experience and feeling, however sad or joyful, however complex and mysterious. The psalms are poetry; they are poetic reflections and insights that emerge, most likely over the centuries, out of a seemingly endless range of human life experience. Because the psalms are poetry, they do not have the usual issues of whether or not they are believable.

Historically the psalms compose a core element in the Bible. Their voice is the voice of reassurance and wisdom. The diversity and spiritual depth of the psalms are testimony to the Bible's ability to nurture and feed the very real spiritual needs of people over the passing centuries.

The psalms cover a range of types: lament, praise, thanksgiving, forgiveness, royal, wisdom, and the songs of Zion of the exilic period. Often, there is some overlapping. Scholars are mostly uncertain about the dating of Psalms, suggesting a period of hundreds of years, dating down to the Exile (587–538 BCE) and beyond. While many of the psalms are traditionally labeled psalms of David, virtually no credible biblical scholar credits David with any authorship.

The spirituality of the psalms recommends them well for liturgical purposes in worship, as well as for wider uses in the spiritual life of the local church. Again, a strength of the psalms is that whatever our life situation, the psalmist has been there. Psalm 100 is one of the most popular psalms, a psalm of praise:

> *Make a joyful noise to the* Lord, *all the earth,*
> *Worship the* Lord *with gladness; come into his presence with singing.*
> *Know that the* Lord *is God. It is he that made us, and we are his; we are*
>   *his people, and the sheep of his pasture.*
>
> (Psalm 100:1–3)

These words of doxology are timeless and reassuring. A poignant psalm of thanksgiving (and of God's forgiving nature) is Psalm 103:

> *Bless the* Lord, *O my soul, and all that is within me, bless his holy*
>   *name.* . . . .
> *The* Lord *is merciful and gracious, slow to anger and abounding in*
>   *steadfast love.*
> *He does not deal with us according to our sins, nor repay us according to*
>   *our iniquities. For as the heavens are high above the earth, so great is*
>   *his steadfast love toward those who fear him.*
>
> (Psalm 103:1, 8, 10–11)

This psalm reveals God's abiding love and forgiving nature. It exudes the psalmist's compassion and love for our human situation. Another psalm of forgiveness is Psalm 51, which is reportedly a psalm of King David in response to his condemnation by the prophet Nathan after David's sinful behavior with Bathsheba and her husband, Uriah the Hittite. The poetry helps us feel the anguish and sense of guilt the psalmist is experiencing:

> *Have mercy upon me, O God, according to your steadfast love; according*
> *to your abundant mercy blot out my transgressions.* . . . . *Create in me a*
> *clean heart, O God, and put a new and right spirit within me.*
>
> (Psalm 51:1, 10)

The psalm below, Psalm 23, overflows with qualitative meaning and memory. We have no doubt heard its melancholic tones in every memorial service or funeral we have attended. Its words remind us that, through whatever comes our way in life, God is with us. We are never alone; God is our eternal companion, our shepherd:

> The LORD is my shepherd, I shall not want. He makes me lie down in green pastures; he leads me beside still waters; he restores my soul. . . . Even though I walk through the darkest valley, I fear no evil; for you are with me; your rod and your staff—they comfort me. (Psalm 23:1–4)

The following verses from Psalm 32 suggest the belief and liberation that come through confession and the unburdening of guilt that is pent up within us. Who among us, at some point, cannot relate to these sensitive words?

> While I kept silence, my body wasted away through my groaning all day long. For day and night your hand was heavy upon me; my strength was dried up as by the heat of summer. Then I acknowledged my sin to you, and I did not hide my iniquity; I said, "I will confess my transgressions to the LORD," and you forgave the guilt of my sin. (Psalm 32:3–5)

Again, as we can see from these psalms, the psalmist has been there. He has walked through the peaks and valleys where we have walked. He feels the nuances of our human struggle for the burdens that come our way in life.

Lastly, a psalm from Israel's experience of exile in Babylon, the darkest hour in Israel's history as a people. We can feel the deep sorrow and melancholy of the moment:

> By the rivers of Babylon—there we sat down and there we wept when we remembered Zion. . . . For there our captors asked us for songs . . . "Sing us one of the songs of Zion!" How could we sing the LORD's song in a foreign land? (Psalm 137:1, 3–4)

See Psalm 139 (page 39) for a psalm on the inescapable God, the inscrutable God who is always with us.

Proverbs

The book of Proverbs is a book of pithy sayings that give simple guidance for how we are to live our lives. We are to follow the way of wisdom. Conveyed through female imagery (commonly known as *Wisdom of God*, or *Sophia*, which is also the Greek word for *wisdom*), following Sophia is the wise way. Contrasted to this is the foolish woman, or the way of the fool.

Proverbs teaches a conventional form of wisdom, namely, that if we abide in the way of wisdom, if we turn away from the way of fools, our lives will go well and the blessings of life will be ours. In other words, honor God, listen to God's teachings and ways, and our days will be good and long upon the earth. Simply put, the way of wisdom leads to life; the way of the fool leads to death.

It is important to note that at this point in Israel's history (although it is difficult to date Proverbs, the completed collection probably came together in the post-exilic period, after 538 BCE), there was no sense of an afterlife. Belief in a heaven or hell beyond death was still three centuries or so into the future.

Proverbs is what Marcus J. Borg calls "conventional wisdom."[1] There are two elements in conventional wisdom. First, in every culture, in every community, it is the wisdom that everybody knows. It is common knowledge, community knowledge, folk knowledge; everybody has it. Second, within this wisdom is the additional knowledge that there are rewards for living right.

If we think about it, it is hard *not* to believe this. We tend to believe that if we live right, if we do all the right things, pay attention to all the right details, do what we are supposed to do, what we know to be the right thing, that our lives will go well. And for the most part, this has probably been our experience. This is the conventional wisdom of the world. It is a performance-and-rewards way of life, deeply embedded in our cultural and religious ways of thinking.

---

[1]Marcus J. Borg, *Reading the Bible Again for the First Time: Taking the Bible Seriously but Not Literally*, (HarperSanFrancisco, 2001), 159.

However, on the underside of this wisdom is the unavoidable question: In our everyday experience, when we live right, have things always worked out for us? While Proverbs is generally unambiguous on this, the books of Ecclesiastes and Job are not. For them, there is an element of randomness to life. Life cannot be so easily reduced to performance and rewards. If this is so, what does this suggest about how we are to live?

Ecclesiastes

What I find compelling about Ecclesiastes is its sobering honesty. The author seems to be a man called Qoheleth, which means "wisdom teacher," who most likely lived in Jerusalem. *Ecclesiastes* is the Greek word for *Qoheleth*. The book is generally dated around 300 to 250 BCE, one of the latest books in the Hebrew Bible.

To begin with, it is amazing that Ecclesiastes is even in the Bible. We don't usually associate the Bible with existential philosophy and skeptical reflections on the meaning or meaninglessness of life. To some observers, Qoheleth would almost seem to be an atheist, so pessimistic are his assessments of his life experiences.

There are two metaphors that appear throughout Ecclesiastes. The first is "vanity of vanities; all is vanity" (Ecclesiastes 1:2). The second is "chasing after wind" (Ecclesiastes 1:14). The term *vanity* suggests words such as breath, vapor, mist, or fog. "All is vanity" becomes "all is breath, or vapor, or mist, or fog," which means all is something hard to grab hold of. Life is so short-lived, so ephemeral; there is nothing of much substance. A "chasing after wind" suggests something eternally elusive, something that we can never catch up to and hold on to.

Qoheleth, it turns out, has done it all:

> So I became great and surpassed all who were before me in Jerusalem. . . . Whatever my eyes desired I did not keep from them; I kept my heart from no pleasure. . . . Then I considered all that my hands had done and the toil I had spent in doing it, and again, all was vanity and

a chasing after wind, and there was nothing to be gained under the sun. (Ecclesiastes 2:9–11)

And then these words of sobering reflection:

So I turned to consider wisdom and madness and folly; for what can the one do who comes after the king? Only what has already been done. (Ecclesiastes 2:12)

Going on—reflecting further—Qoheleth adds:

Yet I perceived that the same fate befalls all of them. Then I said to myself, "What happens to the fool will happen to me also; why then have I been so very wise?" And I said to myself that this also is vanity. . . . So I hated life, because what is done under the sun was grievous to me; for all is vanity and a chasing after wind. (Ecclesiastes 2:14b–15, 17)

And what about the randomness of life?

There is a vanity that takes place on earth, that there are righteous people who are treated according to the conduct of the wicked, and there are wicked people who are treated according to the conduct of the righteous. I said that this also is vanity. (Ecclesiastes 8:14)

And isn't this true in our experience? Good things happen to bad people and bad things to the good. It happens every day. There is no certainty of rewards for performance in life. As we say all the time, stuff happens! It is the way of things!

So what are we to do in life? How are we to live? Qoheleth responds:

Go, eat your bread with enjoyment, and drink your wine with a merry heart; for God has long ago approved what you do. . . . Enjoy life with the wife whom you love, all the days of your vain life that are given you under the sun, because that is your portion in life. . . . Whatever your hand finds to do, do with your might; for there is no work or thought or knowledge or wisdom in Sheol, to which you are going. (Ecclesiastes 9:7, 9–10)

The meaning of life is found in the moment. So quit working so hard to measure up in life! Indeed, stop measuring yourself against everything and everybody! Seize the moment today, right now. Stop all the grasping for one thing or another. *Carpe diem*, seize the day!

Qoheleth is haunted by death. Given the melancholia of his moods, this would scarcely seem to be a surprise:

> *For the fate of humans and the fate of animals is the same; as one dies, so dies the other. They all have the same breath, and humans have no advantage over the animals; for all is vanity. All go to one place; all are from the dust, and all turn to dust again.* (Ecclesiastes 3:19–20)

> *A good name is better than precious ointment, and the day of death, than the day of birth. It is better to go to the house of mourning than to go to the house of feasting, for this is the ending of everyone. . . . The heart of the wise is in the house of mourning.* (Ecclesiastes 7:1–2a, 4a)

The wisdom of Qoheleth runs deep, for, indeed, death is a great teacher. Death is a teacher of true wisdom; death teaches us how to live.

Ecclesiastes challenges the orderly world of conventional wisdom. Its wisdom is a subversive wisdom that makes the settled world of conventional wisdom uneasy.

For example, isn't there an undeniable randomness to life? We just happened to be in the right place at the right time . . . for the right job, the purchase of the right house, meeting up with the right potential spouse. Stuff happens all the time, and a lot of it is random—it just happens.

For Ecclesiastes, God is beyond our ability to domesticate; God is mystery, God is inscrutable. For me, the reflections, ruminations, and insights of Ecclesiastes add immeasurably to the depths and reaches of the Bible. They are so very human, so very real.

Song of Solomon

> *Let him kiss me with the kisses of his mouth! For your love is better than wine.* (Song of Solomon 1:2)

> *Upon my bed at night I sought him whom my soul loves; I sought him, but found him not; I called him, but he gave no answer. . . . Scarcely had I passed them, when I found him whom my soul loves. I held him, and would not let him go until I brought him into my mother's house, and into the chamber of her that conceived me.* (Song of Solomon 3:1, 4)

As these poetic and graphic words suggest, the Song of Solomon is erotic love poetry. How refreshing that these verses of human sexual passion are actually in the Bible. I have a twofold explanation for this.

To begin with, it is more than a little likely that the Song of Solomon was included in the biblical canon because earlier interpreters viewed it as totally allegorical. For these early church leaders, the open expressions of human love were metaphors for God's relationship to Israel (Judaism) and for Christ's relationship to the church (Christianity).

However, beyond this, I like to think that Song of Solomon was included in the canon because of the story it tells. From God's point of view, there is every reason to suggest that human sexuality, at its best, is a beautiful thing, an integral part of the created order that God deemed good in Genesis. Just as creation is good, so are man and woman and their desires for sexual intimacy with one another (this would include homosexual desires for intimacy as well).

What makes the Bible so beautiful (and believable) is exactly this sort of realism. The Bible tells the total story of our human adventure. It reveals the depths of our human strengths and frailties. It asks the tough questions about life and death. Along the way it nudges us to a deeper experience of God and of one another.

For anyone who has ever been passionately in love, Song of Solomon sounds a resonant chord:

You have ravished my heart, my sister, my bride, you have ravished my heart with a glance of your eyes, with one jewel of your necklace. How sweet is your love, my sister, my bride! How much better is your love than wine, and the fragrance of your oils than any spice! Your lips distill nectar, my bride; honey and milk are under your tongue. (Song of Solomon 4:9–11)

Eat, friends, drink, and be drunk with love. I slept, but my heart was awake. Listen! my beloved is knocking. "Open to me, my sister, my love, my dove, my perfect one; for my head is wet with dew, my locks with the drops of the night."

I had put off my garment; how could I put it on again? I had bathed my feet; how could I soil them? My beloved thrust his hand into the opening, and my inmost being yearned for him. I arose to open to my beloved, and my hands dripped with myrrh, my fingers with liquid myrrh, upon the handles of the bolt. I opened to my beloved, but my beloved had turned and was gone. (Song of Solomon 5:1b–6a)

There is something totally unique and sacred about two human beings sharing the erotic and passionate depths of human sexuality. In many ways, such sacred union can be a beautiful blending of our intellectual, spiritual, emotional, and sexual selves. It can be an incredibly rich and intimate sharing. At its best, it can take us to the stars, beyond our words, into the mystery and wonder of life's inexpressible blessedness:

How fair and pleasant you are, O loved one, delectable maiden! You are stately as a palm tree, and your breasts are like its clusters. I say I will climb the palm tree and lay hold of its branches. O may your breasts be like clusters of the vine, and the scent of your breath like apples, and your kisses like the best wine that goes down smoothly, gliding over lips and teeth.

I am my beloved's, and his desire is for me. Come, my beloved, let us go forth into the fields, and lodge in the villages; let us go out early to the vineyards, and see whether the vines have budded, whether the grape blossoms have opened and the pomegranates are in bloom. There I will give you my love. (Song of Solomon 7:6–12)

We do not know who wrote the Song of Solomon. Most likely there were multiple authors. Dating the poetry is also not easy. There are legitimate claims for both pre-exilic and post-exilic authorship. While modern scholarship seems tilted more toward a post-exilic author, there is no clear certainty.

However, what is certain is the impressive diversity of the biblical canon. As I like to say, there is a lot of room in the Bible—room for every conceivable human being, human feeling, human emotion, and human experience; room for the Christian story of grace, mercy, forgiveness, and suffering love; and room for our Creator God who continues to call us into the newness, beauty, love, and mystery that tomorrow promises.

What Job Learned

Simply put, the book of Job is one of the best stories ever told. People of renown and learning, along with humble servants of every stripe, have made this claim for centuries. It is marvelous metaphorical narrative. And it takes us to a place of human humility and insight that hallows our sense of life and God.

The story starts innocently enough with Job, a man blameless and upright in every way; a man, we are told, who "feared God and turned away from evil" (Job 1:1).

One day the heavenly beings came together before God. One of them, Satan, a sort of world ambassador for God, was asked by God what he had been up to.

From going to and fro on the earth [he answered] *and from walking up and down on it.* (Job 1:7)

"Well," said God, "have you considered my servant, Job? There is no one like him on the earth, a blameless and upright man who fears God and turns away from evil" (Job 1:8).

Satan is not impressed. He asks, "Does Job fear God for nothing?" (Job 1:9). Take away some of his endless blessings, Satan offers, and then see what Job does. "He will curse you to your face" (Job 1:11).

"Very well," God agrees. "We shall see; the wager is on. All that [Job] has is in your power; only do not stretch out your hand against him!" (Job 1:12).

In the days ahead, Job begins to lose everything. His children, his servants, all of his herds of animals—all are lost. As if that were not sufficient, soon one infirmity after another attacks Job's body as well. Job's suffering and despair are enormous. What will he do? Where will he turn? His torment seems to have no end.

Beside himself in grief, Job curses the day he was born:

> Let the day perish in which I was born, and the night that said, "A man-child is conceived." Let that day be darkness! May God above not seek it, or light shine on it. Let gloom and deep darkness claim it. Let clouds settle upon it; let the blackness of the day terrify it. (Job 3:3–5)

One of the rhetorical features of Job is the dialogue the author sets before the reader between Job and three of his friends. Ostensibly, his friends—Eliphaz, Bildad, and Zophar—have come to comfort Job and offer him words of solace.

However, his friends have been reared on the performance-and-rewards ethic, a hallmark of the conventional wisdom of the day. Although they no doubt feel bad for Job, they cannot help but think that his misfortune must be related to something he has done. Otherwise what could possibly explain his misery and losses?

One by one his friends try to get Job to acknowledge what wrong he must have done and then to repent for his wrongdoing. Job will have none of it. This is like two incompatible worlds colliding.

Job's friend Eliphaz addresses him:

Think now, who that was innocent ever perished? Or where were the upright cut off? As I have seen, those who plow iniquity and sow trouble reap the same. (Job 4:7–8)

And the words of his friend Bildad pile on:

If you will seek God and make supplication to the Almighty, if you are pure and upright, surely then he will rouse himself for you and restore to you your rightful place. . . . See, God will not reject a blameless person. (Job 8:5–6, 20)

The words of Zophar only add to the indictment:

For you say, "My conduct is pure, and I am clean in God's sight." But O that God would speak, and open his lips to you, and that he would tell you the secrets of wisdom! For wisdom is many-sided. Know then that God exacts of you less than your guilt deserves. (Job 11:4–6)

Clearly Zophar has become impatient with Job. But he goes on:

If you direct your heart rightly, you will stretch out your hands toward him. If iniquity is in your hand, put it far away, and do not let wickedness reside in your tents. Surely then you will lift up your face without blemish; you will be secure, and will not fear. (Job 11:13–15)

Again, Job does not give an inch to his friends. He persists in his declarations of innocence. Flat-out, he thinks they are wrong and misguided. "Worthless physicians" (Job 13:4), he calls them.

In the big picture of things, what is at issue is the inadequacy of conventional wisdom. This wisdom of the world is simply not an adequate explanation for the problem of human suffering. Life is more complicated than that.

It is not always true that if you work hard and do all the right things that life will go well for you. It may; but again, it may not. It is not always the case that if your life is out of joint and not going well that it's your fault and you need to find a way to fix it. Again, it may not be anyone's fault, and it may be a difficult fix. Life is more complicated than a simplistic tit for tat of performance and rewards.

A deeper problem with conventional wisdom is that it doesn't allow for the randomness of life that touches our lives all the time. Sometimes there simply are no easy explanations for things; they just happen. No one is at fault; that is, stuff happens. Like a branch falling on a moving car causing the car to crash into a parked car that was purchased brand-new three days ago. The owner (who was not in the car) is irate, but who's to blame? It just happened.

And so many of the diseases that plague us, along with other physical setbacks, just happen. They are nobody's fault. Oftentimes it is just a random convergence of events, or dispositions, or normal tendencies that create circumstances where the result is cancer. We can only hope it is treatable, which it probably is.

The problem of human suffering, in many situations, has no easy answers. In the book of Job, not only are the author and Job not disciples of conventional wisdom but also neither is God. As the book comes to a close, Job's friends are severely rebuked by God. However, before this ending, Job seeks an encounter with God. The encounter goes well, but it does not turn out the way Job anticipates. In beautiful, poetic speech, God unloads on Job. "Out of the whirlwind," God speaks.

Where were you when I laid the foundations of the earth? (Job 38:4)

Where is the way to the dwelling of light, and where is the place of darkness? (Job 38:19)

Can you hunt the prey for the lion, or satisfy the appetite of the young lions . . . ? Who provides for the raven its prey, when its young ones cry to God, and wander about for lack of food? (Job 38:39, 41)

For four chapters God goes on in this manner. Who, indeed, can fathom the role of the Creator? With marvelous displays of knowledge and vision, God paints a picture of the creation process—the endless creations that God has made, of all forms of life; the immaculate attention to detail; the knowledge behind the knowledge behind the knowledge. It's too much for the human mind to comprehend.

In humility and with a mouth that cannot speak, Job is swept away. Finally, after enough of God's language and Spirit settle in, Job speaks:

> *I know that you can do all things, and that no purpose of yours can be thwarted. "Who is this that hides counsel without knowledge?" Therefore I have uttered what I did not understand, things too wonderful for me, which I did not know. "Hear, and I will speak; I will question you, and you declare to me." (Job 42:2–4)*

In Job's final words he touches on the primary meaning and truth of the entire book. What does this magnificent story teach us?

> *I had heard of you by the hearing of the ear, but now my eye sees you; therefore I despise myself, and repent in dust and ashes. (Job 42:5–6)*

As the book concludes, Job has had a mystical experience, a firsthand experience of God. This makes all the difference. In listening to God out of the whirlwind, Job has crossed over from secondhand to firsthand experience of God. Secondhand experience comes to us from hearing God, through the words of the Bible or the words of some other person. Firsthand experience comes more intuitively from actually seeing God ourselves. In this sense, firsthand experience is mystical in that it is a direct experience of God, much like the mystical experiences of the prophets, for example, or of Jesus and the apostle Paul.

There is a chasm of difference between these two ways of experience. As Marcus J. Borg notes in *Reading the Bible Again for the First Time:*[2]

> *Secondhand religion as religious conventional wisdom is not bad. It can and does produce good. . . . But it is not the same as firsthand religion. The experience of the sacred shatters and transforms secondhand religion.*

---

[2]Marcus J. Borg, *Reading the Bible Again for the First Time: Taking the Bible Seriously but Not Literally* (HarperSanFrancisco, 2001), 179.

The book of Job does not provide any ultimately final answers to the problem of human suffering. But it does give us pause not to be too quick to judge or point the finger (at the poor, for example, or at the marginalized or the unlucky). It also reminds us of the inscrutable mystery of God.

The Gospel Stories

As we think about best stories, the gospels are indeed the best stories we have of our Christian story. They remain *the* primal narrative we know about our faith tradition within Christianity. While the gospels are only minimally historical (meaning a recording of actual historical events), they will forever be our primary source of information about Jesus.

If read metaphorically and understood in light of their historical context, the gospels are eminently believable. However, a metaphorical reading of the texts does not reflect the way the gospels are widely understood in American culture. American culture has pretty much accepted the language of conservative-evangelical Christianity as normative for conversation on our Christian faith.

Many Americans really believe in Jesus' virgin birth and in Mary's immaculate conception. Many really believe in a bodily resurrection and in an afterlife place called heaven. When people hear this language, many do not hear it metaphorically; they hear it in a generally literal way.

For these "many," this is not a problem. But for countless others for whom a literal reading of the Bible doesn't measure up (it is inadequate to our experience), it becomes a major problem. However, rather than thinking it through or seeking out more enlightened interpretations, sadly, many simply reject it and choose to have little to do with the church or the Christian faith.

American culture is hungry for a more progressive and evolved language about our Christian story. This is already happening to varying degrees in some churches and denominations. But the language of these happenings is still not mainstream. Hopefully, over time, this will change; I think it will. If it does not, I believe the church, regrettably, will continue to become less relevant and appealing to legions of people, both in and outside the church.

In the process of affirming the believability of these gospel stories and therefore the importance of reading the Bible (1) metaphorically and (2) in light of its historical context, more and more the Bible begins to make sense. As it does, the stories of the gospels and their teachings increasingly come alive for us.

The gospels were written from approximately 70 to 100 CE. This means they were written some forty to seventy years after Jesus' death and the resurrection experience, however we understand it. If we reflect on this seriously, we can immediately see the challenges we face in our efforts to understand how the gospels are to be read. In the history remembered of the gospels, who knows how many layers of oral tradition (the passing on of events and stories from one person to another) apply? Who knows how the shared memories changed and evolved as the years passed? None of this is to suggest that the gospel stories are not true—true, metaphorically. But it is to question the truth claims of a literal reading of these texts.

We cannot say with any certainty that we know who any of the authors were. Some of the gospel accounts are history remembered, while much of the gospels is history metaphorized (this would apply to virtually all of John).

Most likely the gospel writers were mystics, persons for whom the experience of God, the Spirit, and the sacred was firsthand. Mystics would be particularly adept at metaphorical discourse, which is the only language a mystic has to unpack the depths and nuances of their spiritual awareness and experience. Again, bear in mind that these authors were looking back into history some forty to seventy years in an effort to convey the power, the truth, and the meaning that the post-Easter Jesus had come to hold for them.

In the big picture of things, the gospel writers were trying to be persuasive with a particular community of believers about the larger meaning of Jesus, about who Jesus was for them in their community context. This meant different things for each author.

Let us move now to a look at each of the four gospels. As we do this, I will identify a pivotal opening scene, depicting a deed or action of Jesus that sets the tone for the gospel. These scenes seek to illumine the trajectory of where the gospel story will take us.

Mark

Mark's gospel was most likely written not long after the Roman Empire's destruction of Jerusalem in 70 CE. Thus there was an apocalyptic air hovering over the gospel. In this sense, Mark is the most apocalyptic of the four gospels. Time is of the essence. In such times, repentance (a turning to God) is important.

This theme of repentance recalls the second verse of the gospel where Mark refers to the words of Isaiah 40 (Second Isaiah) during the Babylonian Exile:

> *See, I am sending my messenger ahead of you, who will prepare your way; the voice of one crying out in the wilderness: "Prepare the way of the Lord, make his paths straight."* (Mark 1:2–3)

With this in mind, the pivotal opening scene for Mark is Jesus' first action in Galilee, his proclamation of the good news:

> *The time is fulfilled, and the kingdom of God has come near; repent, and believe in the good news.* (Mark 1:15)

Mark wants to make a connection here between "the way of the Lord" that is a return from exile, and the way of Jesus which, for Mark, is the way of suffering love that leads to resurrection. Repentance is a turning back, a returning from exile.

As the gospel story moves along, powerful apocalyptic tones are sounded again in Mark 13. As Jesus is leaving the Temple, one of his disciples comments to him about the large stones and large buildings. Mark, then, has Jesus say to him:

Do you see these great buildings? Not one stone will be left here upon another; all will be thrown down. (Mark 13:2)

Later, his disciples ask him:

When will this be, and what will be the sign that these things are about to be accomplished? (Mark 13:4)

Jesus then warns them of false teachers, future wars, and natural disasters. He warns them as well of the gruesome persecution that they will encounter. Finally, he tells them:

But when you see the desolating sacrilege set up where it ought not to be (let the reader understand), then those in Judea must flee to the mountains. (Mark 13:14)

Reference to the "desolating sacrilege" clearly refers to what the Roman Empire just did to the Jewish Temple in Jerusalem (they desecrated and destroyed it). This apocalyptic eschatology in Mark prompts the Jesus of Mark's gospel to respond:

But in those days, after the suffering, the sun will be darkened, and the moon will not give its light, and the stars will be falling from heaven, and the powers in the heavens will be shaken. Then they will see "the Son of Man coming in the clouds" with great power and glory. Then he will send out the angels, and gather his elect from the four winds, from the ends of the earth to the ends of heaven. (Mark 13:24–27)

In this context, where apocalyptic language and imagery is at the forefront— for obvious reasons, that is, the desolation of the war with Rome—the call to repentance and a return from exile is important. The call to a life of suffering love unto death looms real.

Metaphorically, for the author of Mark's gospel, the way of the cross is a dying to an old way of being and an opening to a new way of life through discipleship to Jesus.

Matthew

Matthew's gospel was probably written some ten to fifteen years after Mark (around 80–85 CE). For the author of Matthew, Mark was a critical source. Matthew had two additional sources, Q (for the German, *quelle*, which means "source") and his own sources, which we'll call M.

To begin with, Matthew's gospel is the most Jewish of the four gospels. Indeed, from the first verses in chapter one, in the genealogy of Jesus, Matthew links Jesus to Abraham, the traditional father of Judaism.

Matthew seems to have a complicated relationship to Judaism. On the one hand, he is decidedly Jewish and considers belief in Jesus to be a natural unfolding within Judaism. For him, being a follower of Jesus is what being a good Jew leads to. Thus, in seeking to connect Jewish beliefs to belief in Jesus, Matthew quotes the Hebrew Bible again and again (around forty times in all). (We should note that Christianity, as a distinct religion, wasn't born until probably the middle of the second century. Early on, therefore, virtually all of Jesus' followers were Jews.) Indeed, in Matthew 5, the author has Jesus say:

> *Do not think that I have come to abolish the law or the prophets; I have come not to abolish but to fulfill.* (Matthew 5:17)

On the other hand, Matthew reveals an open hostility to the Jewish leaders who continue to reject Jesus—even to the point of throwing Jesus-believing Jews out of the synagogues. Later in the gospel (chapter 23), Matthew unleashes an indicting invective against the scribes and Pharisees when he has Jesus say:

> *But woe to you, scribes and Pharisees, hypocrites! For you lock people out of the kingdom of heaven. . . . Woe to you scribes and Pharisees, hypocrites! For you cross the sea and land to make a single convert, and you make the new convert twice as much a child of hell as yourselves.* (Matthew 23:13, 15)

"Blind fools," he calls them, as the woes go on. Seven consecutive *woes* mark this twenty-third chapter, culminating in these harsh words:

You snakes, you brood of vipers! How can you escape being sentenced to hell? (Matthew 23:33)

The context for this very deep tension is that after the destruction of the Temple in 70 CE by the Romans, the center of Jewish life no longer existed. In order to sustain community life and identity, therefore, Jewish leaders began the practice of ostracizing Jesus-believing Jews, claiming they were no longer true Jews. Of course, Matthew's position on this was the opposite: that Jesus-believing Jews were precisely the ones being faithful to the traditions of Israel.

The pivotal opening scene in Matthew's gospel is the Sermon on the Mount (chapters 5–7), where the author's presentation of Jesus clearly reflects a Moses typology. Moses is the most revered prophet/leader in all of the Hebrew Bible. His spirit and accomplishments loom over the history and traditions of Israel like none other.

Whereas Moses ascended to Mount Sinai to receive the Ten Commandments, Jesus climbs a hill to teach his followers, starting out with the Beatitudes (comparable to the Ten Commandments). For Matthew, Jesus is one like Moses. Just as the Ten Commandments are a core teaching of Israel (part of the Pentateuch, Israel's primal narrative), the Sermon on the Mount captures the best teachings of Jesus in the New Testament's primal narrative.

Matthew's passion and inclusive spirit continue to shine through the challenges of life within his community. His gospel closes with what is known as the Great Commission, again, received by his disciples on a mountain:

Go therefore and make disciples of all nations, baptizing them in the name of the Father and of the Son and of the Holy Spirit, and teaching them to obey everything that I have commanded you. And remember, I am with you always, to the end of the age. (Matthew 28:19–20)

Again, read metaphorically, as history metaphorized, Matthew's gospel is a powerful story. From the birth narrative, through the high-ground message in the Sermon on the Mount, on through the different parables and teachings to the events of Holy Week and the Great Commission, the message of inclusive love echoes through the pages. More on much of this in chapter 5, "The Jesus You Didn't Know You Could Believe In."

Luke-Acts

The Gospel of Luke was most likely written some ten to twenty years after the Gospel of Mark (80–90 CE). Luke, who might have been a Gentile convert, also wrote the Acts of the Apostles. For his gospel, Luke had both Mark and Q as sources, along with his own source, which we'll call L.

Luke's is the gospel with the most parables, numbering fifteen, among which are some of the best parables Jesus gave us (e.g., the parables of the good Samaritan, the prodigal son, and the talents). Luke's gospel also has the most healings and advocacy for the poor, the sick, and the marginalized. More still, Luke has more women depicted in his gospel than the other gospel writers.

As the pivotal opening scene from Luke 4 suggests, Luke's gospel has the strongest emphasis on social justice of the gospels. As the story goes:

> When he came to Nazareth, where he had been raised, he went into the synagogue on the sabbath day, as was his custom. He stood up to read, and the scroll from the prophet Isaiah was given to him. He unrolled the scroll and found the place where it was written:
>
> The Spirit of the Lord is upon me, because he has anointed me to bring good news to the poor. He has sent me to proclaim release to the captives and recovery of sight to the blind, to let the oppressed go free, and to proclaim the year of the Lord's favor. (Luke 4:16–19)

This language from Isaiah 61, known as Third Isaiah (Isaiah 56–66 BCE), sets the tone splendidly for what lies ahead in Luke's gospel. Jesus, it seems, is always healing someone: he performs healings at Simon's house (Luke 4:38–39ff.), cleanses a leper (5:12–13ff.), heals a paralytic (5:18–25ff.), heals a man with a withered hand (6:6–10ff.), heals a centurion's servant (7:2–10ff.), raises a widow's son (7:12–15ff.), forgives a woman sinner (7:37–48ff.), heals a demoniac

(8:27–39ff.), heals a hemorrhaging woman (8:43–48ff.), and restores a girl to life (8:41–42, 49–56ff.).

And this is only in chapters 4 through 8. Later in this same chapter 4, Jesus talks about two Hebrew prophets, Elijah and Elisha, who were sent to Gentiles—Elijah to provide food for a widow at Zarephath, and Elisha to heal the leper, Naaman, a Syrian. Although this action angered Jesus' hometown folks, it nonetheless reveals Luke's inclusive, universal impulse.

In Luke and Acts, the Spirit is an active player and is a source of ongoing inspiration and empowerment. In Luke's birth narrative, the Spirit not only nurtures the birth of Jesus but also fills Zechariah and Elizabeth, the parents of John the Baptist, as well. Soon after Jesus' birth, guided by the Spirit, an old man named Simeon comes into the Temple; and when Jesus' parents bring the infant Jesus in for a blessing required under the law, Simeon takes him in his arms and praises God, saying:

> *Master, now you are dismissing your servant in peace, according to your word; for my eyes have seen your salvation, which you have prepared in the presence of all peoples, a light for revelation to the Gentiles and for glory to your people Israel.* (Luke 2:29–32)

In Acts, Luke's account of the development of the early church—first within Judaism and then with the wider Gentile world—he tells the story of Pentecost, the coming of the Holy Spirit on the gathered faithful in Jerusalem. The trajectory of the story is a reversal of the story of the Tower of Babel. In the latter account, the tongues of the people are confused by the Spirit to where they cannot understand one another. In the coming of the Spirit at Pentecost, the people are all speaking in different tongues but are able to understand each other.

The Spirit continues to be an active participant throughout the book of Acts. It helps the disciple Philip minister to an Ethiopian eunuch (Acts 8); it sustains Paul in his Damascus Road conversion experience (Acts 9); and it is with Peter in his conversion experience in Caesarea. Through the Spirit, Gentile after Gentile is able to hear the early church's stories of Jesus and is invited to become a part of the fledgling Christian community.

The inclusive spirit of compassion and social justice that runs through Luke's gospel suggests that Luke was familiar with the prophetic work of Second Isaiah (Isaiah 40–55), particularly Isaiah 53, the well-known chapter on the suffering servant. In the Emmaus Road Easter story in Luke 24, Jesus appears in spirit to two disconsolate believers on the road to the village of Emmaus. Engaging them in conversation, he reminds them:

> *Was it not necessary that the Messiah should suffer these things and then enter into his glory?* (Luke 24:26)

None of these accounts are literally historical, of course. They are metaphorical narratives mixed with perhaps some history remembered. Yet they are truthful stories about the power of the Spirit and inclusive love to draw people in and to lift them to a larger vision of the possibilities for the life of faith in the evolving Christian movement.

John

Most biblical scholars date the Gospel of John to the late first century and early second century (around 100 CE). As with the other gospels, there is no certainty about authorship. For a time, scholars attributed the gospel to the disciple John, the son of Zebedee; still others thought the enigmatic "beloved disciple" (introduced in chapter 13) might be the author. Although modern scholars do not claim to know the gospel's author, they believe that as many as three to possibly five authors were involved.

As the most distinct of the four gospels, John has no nativity story, no parables, and no Last Supper and Gethsemane experiences. John shares two miracles with the other gospels: the feeding of the five thousand and Jesus walking on water. And while there is no Last Supper, John has Jesus washing the feet of the disciples (chapter 13), a sacred act in its own right.

Part of the uniqueness of the Gospel of John is that, most likely, none of the events recorded in the gospel are actual historical happenings. John's gospel, therefore, is virtually all metaphorical narrative, the creation of its multiple authors.

The gospel is like a long poem, so rich is its language, so probing are its insights. Take the prologue, for example. Listen to these opening words:

> *In the beginning was the Word, and the Word was with God, and the Word was God. He was in the beginning with God. All things came into being through him, and without him not one thing came into being. What has come into being in him was life, and the life was the light of all people. The light shines in the darkness, and the darkness did not overcome it.* (John 1:1–5)

The poetic voice here (some think John's prologue is based on Proverbs 8:22ff.) is utterly captivating. Immediately we are drawn in, eager to discover what is to follow. Beyond the beautiful language, the prologue serves to connect Jesus to the dawn of creation, lending a universal ring to the gospel message.

The metaphorical excellence of John's gospel is also helpful in another way. It invites us to glimpse the mystery of God and the Spirit. We see this also in the famous I AM statements that I will say more about later. Noting the hypnotic poetry, along with the element of mystery that looms over the gospel, the author of John was probably the most mystical of the gospel writers.

Again, mystics are persons who have experiences of God, the Spirit, and the holy. Mystics *know* God in an experiential way and have frequent firsthand experiences of the sacred. There is little doubt, for example, that Jesus was a mystic. (More on this in our chapter on Jesus.) Both the prologue, the I AM statements, and different elements of the discourse speeches (John 13–17) include language and ideas on which a mystic might reflect and meditate.

For example, note again Jesus' words to Martha before raising Lazarus to life:

> *I am the resurrection and the life. Those who believe in me, even though they die, will live, and everyone who lives and believes in me will never die. Do you believe this?* (John 11:25–26)

These words immediately invite the mystic to engage and plug in. Or take these lofty words from John 7:

On the last day of the festival, the great day, while Jesus was standing there, he cried out, "Let anyone who is thirsty come to me, and let the one who believes in me drink. As the scripture has said, 'Out of the believer's heart, shall flow rivers of living water.'" (John 7:37–38)

Certainly all of this is food for thought and reflection, as the Spirit moves. The pivotal opening scene for John is the wedding at Cana, from John 2. At this famous wedding, when the wine is running out, Jesus moves into action. Seeing six huge stone water jars near by, he tells the servants to fill the jars with water. He then tells them to draw some water out and take it to the chief steward.

The steward, noting that the water was wine, is in disbelief. He has no idea where the wine came from. Calling the bridegroom, he says to him:

Everyone serves the good wine first, and then the inferior wine after the guests have become drunk. But you have kept the good wine until now. (John 2:10)

So what are we to make of this? Clearly it is a symbolic event, but what does it mean?

To begin with, wedding banquets were the most celebrative occasions in first-century Palestine. Normally people's diets were somewhat bland, seldom including meat, for example. But at wedding banquets there were copious amounts of all kinds of food, and the party lasted for seven days. Again, these were notably festive events.

Having said this, what does John mean by putting this wedding event so early in his gospel? What is a life with Jesus about? What does it mean to be in John's faith community? What it means is that being a disciple of Jesus is like being at a party where the wine never runs out and they save the best until last. In other words: What a party! What a life!

Finally, what are the well-known I AM verses about? What are we to make of them?

I am the bread of life! (John 6:35)
I am the light of the world! (John 8:12)
I am the good shepherd! (John 10:11)
I am the resurrection and the life! (John 11:25, 26)
I am the way, the truth and the life! (John 14:6)
I am the vine, you are the branches! (John 15:5)

While there is no conclusive explanation for the I AM sayings in John, it is interesting to think of them in relation to God's reply to Moses in Exodus 3:13 when Moses asks God:

If I come to the Israelites and say to them, "The God of your ancestors has sent me to you," and they ask me, "What is his name?" what shall I say to them?

God answers Moses, saying:

"I AM WHO I AM." He said further, "Thus you shall say to the Israelites, 'I AM has sent me to you.'" (Exodus 3:13–14)

There is a profound element of mystery and wonder in God's response. My sense of this is that our human attempt to name God or describe God is beyond words. We simply have no words that are adequate to the challenge. God is always beyond (more than, greater than) our human ability to define God or describe God. God is ineffable, always more than we can imagine.

By linking Jesus' language in his gospel to the I AM language in Exodus 3 with Moses, John is seeking to tie Jesus to God in the sense of the deep awe, respect, and esteem we hold for him. Also, we can say that Jesus is all these things (e.g., the bread of life, good shepherd, light of the world, etc.) in ways and with meanings that we cannot fully grasp. And because he is all of this and more, he is deserving of our most ardent discipleship and love.

Paul

The life, mission, and writings of the apostle Paul loom large over the Christian church. Whatever our personal opinion of Paul, after Jesus, he is *the* major personality in the shaping and growth of the early church. His contribution to Christianity is immeasurable by almost any standard.

Given what Paul has meant to Christianity, his story is clearly one of the best stories of the Hebrew/Christian Bible. When we think about believability, about how believable Paul is, we have some sorting out to do.

Paul's authentic letters (termed *epistles*), which number seven—Romans, 1 and 2 Corinthians, Galatians, Philippians, 1 Thessalonians, and Philemon—were most likely written from 51 to 62 CE, with 1 Thessalonians coming first and Philippians last. The letters were often complicated responses to actual, sometimes pressing problems in the churches he had helped start up. Still, they were letters in *real* time, which means they were not written some forty years or more after the fact, like the gospels.

Context

Certainly the letters are believable in that they really happened. The challenge is more a question of understanding them, and for this, historical context is everything. Paul's communications to the churches were highly contextual; they grew out of (1) his relationship to the churches and (2) the social-cultural values of first-century Palestine. The one exception was Romans, a church he had not yet visited when he wrote the letter.

While much of Paul's communication makes use of metaphor and symbolic language, historical context is even more important. For example, take Paul's counsel in 1 Corinthians 7 concerning marriage:

> *Now concerning the matters about which you wrote: "It is well for a man not to touch a woman." But because of cases of sexual immorality, each man should have his own wife and each woman her own husband. The*

husband should give to his wife her conjugal rights, and likewise the wife to her husband. For the wife does not have authority over her own body, but the husband does; likewise the husband does not have authority over his own body, but the wife does. (1 Corinthians 7:1–4)

For the implications of this text, once again, context is everything:

- Given Paul's reputation with some for being hard on women, this reading would seem to have a remarkably egalitarian message. There is virtually no distinction here between the proper roles of husbands and wives in a marital relationship. This is but one of numerous incidents when, in reality, Paul comes across as a relative progressive in his views on women. Indeed, in the first century, generally, women were treated as second- or third-class citizens, with virtually no rights of their own. Again, the importance of context!

- In the next couple verses, Paul admits that he would prefer husbands and wives to be like he is (Paul is not married), which would be to refrain from any sexual activity. One reason he urges such abstinence is because of his belief (and the belief of many in the early days of the first-century church) in Jesus' imminent return. Once more, context is so important.

As we consider Paul's apostolic role, think of the enormous challenge before him. He was *the* singular pathfinder in the shaping of the early church. There was no precedent church experience for him to learn from. There was no manual on church organizational structure and protocol for leader-member conduct. Paul had to learn and lead on the fly, so to speak.

Thus we can imagine the incredible importance for some level of uniformity and internal consistency on what the churches were teaching about Jesus and the meaning of his crucifixion and resurrection. And what about questions of believers' personal behavior as well as guidelines for the way believers practiced their faith within the church community?

For example, in partaking of the Lord's Supper, abuses were reported in the church:

For when the time comes to eat, each of you goes ahead with your own supper, and one goes hungry and another becomes drunk. What! Do you not have homes to eat and drink in? Or do you show contempt for the church of God and humiliate those who have nothing? (1 Corinthians 11:21–22)

Then a few verses later:

Whoever, therefore, eats the bread or drinks the cup of the Lord in an unworthy manner will be answerable for the body and blood of the Lord. Examine yourselves, and only then eat of the bread and drink of the cup. (1 Corinthians 11:27–28)

The point in all of this is that context (historical, social, and cultural) plays a significant role in determining the tone and the substance of Paul's letters. Speaking of context, in order to better understand Paul, it is important that we try to grasp the transformative significance of his Damascus Road conversion. Whatever this experience was, it totally changed Paul's personal identity and life purpose.

Damascus Road

While Paul's Damascus Road conversion most likely took place some five years after Jesus' death (around 35 CE), Paul's letters, again, are generally dated from 51 to 62 CE. We presume that the period of some fifteen years between his conversion and the beginning of his letter-writing activity was a time when the earliest churches were starting up.

Paul's activity as the apostle to the Gentiles began with his Damascus Road experience (Acts 9). While often referred to as a conversion experience, it was more of a conversion *within* Judaism, to another way of being Jewish. Paul was always a Jew first; that was simply who he was. His commitment to Christ and to the way of Jesus was an outgrowth (an emergent) of his Judaism.

Paul's Damascus Road experience (some form of mystical transformation) totally changed him and redirected his life purpose. Before his conversion, Paul, a Pharisee, had been a zealous persecutor of new followers of the way (i.e., of early Christianity, although the term *Christianity* had not yet emerged). However, now, on the Damascus Road, suddenly:

> *a light from heaven flashed around him. He fell to the ground and heard a voice saying to him, "Saul, Saul, why do you persecute me?"* (Acts 9:3–4)

When Paul asked, "Who are you, Lord?" The reply came:

> *"I am Jesus, whom you are persecuting. But get up and enter the city, and you will be told what you are to do."* (Acts 9:5–6)

Soon after learning of the Lord's intent, Paul's new life as an apostle to the Gentiles was born:

> *He [Paul] is an instrument whom I have chosen to bring my name before Gentiles and kings and before the people of Israel.* (Acts 9:15)

Throughout Paul's active missionary work, his Damascus Road experience remained central to his identity as an apostle of Christ. It was the closest he came to an actual experience of Jesus in the flesh. Later, in his important interactions with the pillars of the Jerusalem church (Peter, James, and John), Paul always felt somewhat diminished because he had *not* known Jesus in the same way they had (in the flesh).

> *He appeared to Cephas, then to the twelve. Then he appeared to more than five hundred brothers and sisters. . . . Then he appeared to James, then to all the apostles. Last of all, as to one untimely born, he appeared also to me. For I am the least of the apostles.* (1 Corinthians 15:5–9a)

So what did Paul teach, preach, and believe? For Paul, throughout his ministry, the central message of his preaching evolved out of his Damascus Road mystical experience. For him, the living Christ he encountered that day continued to be the cornerstone of what he preached and believed.

Jesus Is Lord

The status of Jesus as Lord was very important to Paul. For him, *Lord* was a title of the deepest honor and respect. Also, it meant that other gods, idols, and kings were *not* Lord; Jesus was Lord. In the popular culture of the day, the term *Lord* suggested the master of a slave or a reference to a king or a person in a high position of authority.

Again, historical context is important in our understanding of the term's usage. I am uncomfortable with the way the term *Lord* is used in our contemporary faith language. It seems to move Jesus closer to the status of God, which I would not want to do. Still, for Paul in his context, the term has meaning related to his Damascus Road experience. For him, Jesus is Lord.

One of the most poetic and powerful uses of *Lord* for Paul is in his letter to the Philippians:

> *Let the same mind be in you that was in Christ Jesus, who, though he was in the form of God, did not regard equality with God as something to be exploited, but emptied himself, taking the form of a slave, being born in human likeness. And being found in human form, he humbled himself and became obedient to the point of death—even death on a cross.*

> *Therefore God also highly exalted him and gave him the name that is above every name, so that at the name of Jesus every knee should bend, in heaven and on earth . . . and every tongue confess that Jesus Christ is Lord, to the glory of God.* (2:5–11)

"In Christ"

Again, Paul's Damascus Road experience convinced him that he (Paul) was now "in Christ." The "in Christ" metaphor is contrasted to being "in Adam," or "of the world." Adam had yielded to the serpent in the garden and now the sin of the world was in him. To be "in Adam" is to be dead to the world; to be "in Christ" is to be alive to the promises of God.

The language of "in Christ" is also suggestive of the "new creation," as distinguished from the old. 2 Corinthians encourages us:

> *So if anyone is in Christ, there is a new creation: everything old has passed away; see, everything has become new! All this is from God, who reconciled us to himself through Christ.* (5:17–18)

The "in Christ" language is reflective of the battle in our spirit between good and evil:

> *For I do not do what I want, but I do the very thing I hate. . . . I can will what is right, but I cannot do it. For I do not do the good I want, but the evil I do not want is what I do. Now if I do what I do not want, it is no longer I that do it, but sin that dwells within me.* (Romans 7:15, 18–20)

Life in Adam is the impulse that nudges us off track and leads to death. It is the contrast to this, the life in Christ, that leads us to live in God's ways, the ways of kindness and humility, love and compassion, with joyful and gracious spirits.

Christ language leaves some people cold, as if not knowing what it is supposed to mean; it seems somehow too exalted and in some way less than real. *Christ* is Greek for the Hebrew word *Messiah*, the anointed one of God. The term need not be equated with God. More correctly, for Christians, Jesus is God's Christ, or God's Messiah; again, the anointed one of God. For me, it is important *not* to equate Jesus with God. Indeed, who is Jesus then? Jesus is God's Messiah.

Justification by Grace

The *justification-by-grace* metaphor is one of the core teachings in Paul's faith. It is something he has personally known firsthand. His experience of the risen Christ was clearly, for him, an act of God's grace.

The question is, how are we put right with God? As human beings, imperfect and not without sin, how are we reconciled to the Creator? Paul argues vehemently that it is not by works and not through the law. Rather, it is by grace and through faith. In this sense, we do not earn God's love or God's favor; God extends it to us freely—as we are—as an act of grace.

God's grace is about our relationship to God in the present. Again, it is not something we earn through hard work or right belief. God accepts us as we are, no questions asked. We are accepted, valued, and justified by grace. Justification by grace is revealing of the character and nature of God:

> *Now we know that whatever the law says, it speaks to those who are under the law, so that every mouth may be silenced, and the whole world may be held accountable to God. For "no human being will be justified in his sight" by deeds prescribed by the law. . . . Since all have sinned and fallen short of the glory of God; they are now justified by his grace as a gift.* (Romans 3:19–20, 23–24)

If we are paying attention, this is a radical message. The freedom of God's grace reaches out to all human beings—the good and the bad, the diligent and the indifferent. Justification by grace is a protest against all legalisms. Moreover, it has nothing to do with heaven; it is about life in the present.

Justification by grace would seem to run counter to a lot of the religion we see practiced in our nation. We are such a performance-reward culture. Church folks nod their head to the justification-by-grace sermon, but they quickly return to the performance-reward drumbeat of the workplace that sets the tone for so much of our modern living.

Christ Crucified

The graphic metaphor of *Christ crucified* is almost too much. It is such a powerful symbol, not a reality any of us would want to experience any time soon. To begin with, it presents an apparent contradiction. How could God's Christ get crucified? Assuming God to be a powerful God, it makes no sense. Such a crucifixion would seem to signal an ending, not a beginning. Yet over time, Easter came, followed by the day of Pentecost, and the church was born.

Christ crucified points to the suffering love of both Jesus and God. It evokes images and language of the suffering servant in Isaiah 53:

> *But he was wounded for our transgressions, crushed for our iniquities; upon him was the punishment that made us whole, and by his bruises we are healed. All we like sheep have gone astray; we have all turned to our own way, and the LORD has laid on him the iniquity of us all.* (Isaiah 53:5–6)

The vivid poetry of this Isaiah 53 servant song introduces a new awareness to the people of Israel. The destruction and devastation of the Exile changed Israel forever. So great were her losses, she needed to embrace a new metaphor to move forward. That metaphor, detailed is Isaiah 53, was of the suffering servant. It was a metaphor of stark humbleness of spirit and suffering love.

Suffering love is not a weak love. Quite the contrary. It points to a way of being where every nation, tribe, and person are seen, heard, and valued. Suffering love is scary stuff. It cannot be bought or sold; it is hardly marketable. It is the foolishness of God that is the wisdom of God.

Against its stand, the domination systems of the world are powerless, not knowing where to turn. Suffering love can redeem the world, any time, any day, any place.

Christ crucified reveals the pale wisdom of the world. It is like a mirror for the world to see who it is and what it has become. Earlier, to Israel in exile, the prophet says:

> *I am the LORD, I have called you to righteousness, I have taken you by the hand and kept you; I have given you as a covenant to the people, a light to the nations, to open the eyes that are blind.* (Isaiah 42:6–7a)

Christ crucified gives new perspective to everything we are and do in life. The power and mystery of the reality to which it points hover over us always, inviting us to higher spiritual ground.

Body of Christ and Social Justice

The *body of Christ* is Paul's image for the church, much as the kingdom of God is Jesus' image. Both metaphors extend extravagant welcomes; they invite us in.

In our celebration of the Lord's Supper, in the breaking of the bread, we are reminded how we stand in solidarity with one another, each of us a part of the body of Christ that is the church. The implication is powerful: We are all in this life together. We are all part of the human family, all precious in the sight of God.

The body of Christ is an inclusive community of God's people. In this body, all barriers and dividers are broken down and removed. Listen to Paul in Galatians:

> *There is no longer Jew or Greek, there is no longer slave or free, there is no longer male and female; for all of you are one in Christ Jesus.* (3:28)

The letters of Paul overflow with pleas for patience, kindness, and love. Paul is always thinking about the big picture of his mission. At the end of the day, Paul knows: it is all about the love. And about this love, Paul writes some of the most beautiful poetry we know. Talk about best stories! 1 Corinthians 13 overflows.

1 Corinthians 13

Given what we know of Paul, even with his marvelous intellect, it is still stunning that he is the author of 1 Corinthians 13. In my forty some years of ministry, I have probably performed more than twelve hundred weddings. In virtually every one of these weddings, words from this captivating poem were read at some point.

This poem has it all. It is dramatic and compelling; it is emphatic and challenging:

> *If I speak in the tongues of mortals and of angels, but do not have love, I am a noisy gong or a clanging cymbal. And if I have prophetic powers, and understand all mysteries and all knowledge, and if I have all faith,*

so as to remove mountains, but do not have love, I am nothing. If I give away all my possessions, and if I hand over my body so that I may boast, but do not have love, I gain nothing. (1 Corinthians 13:1–3)

The drama builds, the mystery heightens. Indeed, love is really something to behold. Paul then talks about the ways of love, culminating with how love

bears all things, believes all things, hopes all things, endures all things. (1 Corinthians 13:7)

And then the climatic three words: "Love never ends." The poem concludes by inviting us on a journey of life's deep transitions leading to a mystical awakening:

Now I know only in part; then I will know fully, even as I have been fully known. And now faith, hope and love abide, these three; and the greatest of these is love. (1 Corinthians 13:12–13)

Indeed, how believable is this Bible? Believable indeed!

BIBLE STORIES HELP TELL US WHO WE ARE

As we begin to find ourselves in the stories of the Bible, we learn early on that there is a lot of room in the Bible—room to be human, which means room to fail and succeed, to mourn and celebrate; room for sadness and joy, for belief and doubt; room to die and room to live. In this sense we find ourselves in the Bible and the Bible, over time, helps tell us who we are.

It is one of the subordinate theses of this book that when we use our minds in a probing and disciplined way, when we humbly seek to understand how the Bible was formed and how it came together as both Hebrew and Christian Scriptures, as both Old Testament and New Testament canon; when we take seriously the importance of historical context and a metaphorical reading of the biblical texts, it is easier for us to believe and to give witness to our belief.

FROM GENERATION TO GENERATION, HOW THE BIBLE HAS LIVED ON

In our reflections on the Bible, it should also be noted that there is something almost sacred about the Bible's durability, about how it has endured all these years. It has been reprinted in virtually every language on the planet. Through the efforts of the Gideons and others, copies of the Bible can be found in most hotel rooms across our country. Countless thousands of churches across the world offer frequent Bible study groups throughout the calendar year. These same churches read from the Bible in their weekly (or daily) services of worship. In other words, the Bible remains abundantly present in much of our community life across the earth.

Because the Bible has survived all these years, decades, and centuries, it is deserving of a certain respect and dignity. These best stories we know of the Bible have imparted faith and meaning to untold millions over time, to where the Bible deserves, minimally, some hearing in our lives. The truth claims of the Bible, whether we agree with them or not, merit our consideration.

One of the goals of this book is to present the Bible in a way that, while being honest about its origins and imperfections, is not too quickly dismissed as outdated and irrelevant for our modern world. Along these lines, we have to ask ourselves (with humble spirits), what is it about these faith stories, about the truth claims of the Bible, that has enabled it to live on all these years?

Put another way, why do we continue to tell these stories? Why do these faith narratives, parables, and poems (e.g., the Psalms) continue to be read and referenced in the most sacred and important settings of our communal lives?

Clearly these biblical stories and teachings have survived because, over time, they have continued to offer meaning and truth to our personal and communal lives. In and through these stories we have continued to find our identity. In this sense, the Bible has helped shape us and tell us who we are. When we say "these are the best stories we know," it means something. It means something because the stories and teachings continue to feed us, nurture us, and shape us. In the big picture of things, the Bible and its teachings and wisdom are adequate to our modern experience. However, for this adequacy to be sustained, the Bible must be freed from the constraints of biblical literalism.

WHERE THE BIBLE POINTS US

When we move beyond a literal reading of the scriptures, increasingly we will be able to be persuasive with people about the truth and power of the biblical message. When the Bible is not read as history, nor as science, nor as a factual accounting, but rather as the spiritual story of God and God's people; when the Bible is seen as a profoundly human document (not perfect, but abundantly rich in relational love, wisdom, and meaning), the depth and reaches of its teachings will draw people in. People will be moved and they will want to learn more.

I have no doubt about the Bible's profound wisdom, truth, and meaning. The richness of the biblical stories is virtually boundless. Again and again the Bible enlightens us and challenges us on the depths of who we are. It does this through history remembered and metaphorical narrative. It does this through mystical probing and poetic insight. For the stories of the Bible to be woven through the myths of antiquity need not pose a problem. For the question that most concerns us is not "Did this really happen?" but rather "What does it mean?"

From the temptations of Adam and Eve in the garden, the stories of Noah and the flood, and the Tower of Babel, to the faith revealed in Abraham and Sarah, to the ongoing challenge of God's covenant with the patriarchs; through Moses and the giving of the Law, through the flawed humanity of King David (Israel's greatest king); through the suffering and courage of the prophets and of Israel in exile, the values and truths of the biblical story march on.

Once again we are invited to find ourselves in the story. We are invited to learn, grow, and open ourselves with largeness of heart to the life-giving power of the Spirit.

WHAT THE BIBLE UNDERSTANDS

More than we may want to know, the Bible understands. While Israel's greatest era was the reign of King David (who himself was profoundly human), Israel's most notorious low was the sin-plagued events leading up to the Exile, followed by the years of suffering in Babylon (587–538 BCE). Indeed, during this exilic period, the challenge of the priestly writers was to find some way of explaining the horrific devastation of the Exile experience.

As I noted earlier, Israel lost everything at the hands of the Babylonians. The monarch, deported; Jerusalem, destroyed; the Temple, destroyed; the Torah, carried off; the people, the elites, deported, leaving only the peasants behind. How could this have happened? How does Israel explain this to herself? How is Israel to understand this in light of her history as God's chosen people? And finally, how is Israel to relate this to future generations?

The two most significant events in the Hebrew Bible are the Exodus and the Exile. The Exodus from Egypt remained a cornerstone of Israel's faith and hope. It evoked vivid memories of the God who heard Israel crying out, rescued the Israelites from the oppressive hand of Pharaoh, had compassion for her pain, and stuck with her through the highs and lows of her wilderness experience en route to the promised land.

The Exile was another story. As suggested earlier, this was Israel's worst nightmare. God had pronounced God's protest for years through prophetic voices. Yet disobedience and corruption were everywhere. There was arrogance in high places, exploitation of the poor and injustice all about. At last, the hand of doom had fallen and it fell hard.

Israel spent almost fifty years in exile in Babylon. Forced to adjust to a new way of life, early on she was confused and crushed by the doom that had befallen her. The Bible does not cover over this national tragedy. The Bible knows; Israel's suffering was severe. To be truthful, even though a few thousand Israelites returned during what is known as the restoration (after 538 BCE), Israel was never the same.

The Bible abounds with human stories: stories of imperfection and demise, stories of darkness and death, but stories, too, of reconciliation and peace, compassion and love. It's the human story.

And so it is, from these first words of Genesis, the Bible's first holy words:

> *In the beginning when God created the heavens and the earth, the earth was a formless void and darkness covered the face of the deep, while a wind from God swept over the face of the waters. Then God said, "Let there be light"; and there was light.* (Genesis 1:1–3)

and through the poetic words in the closing chapters of Revelation:

> *Then I saw a new heaven and a new earth; for the first heaven and the first earth had passed away. . . . And I saw the holy city, the new Jerusalem, coming down out of heaven from God. . . . And I heard a loud voice from the throne saying, "See, the home of God is among mortals. He will dwell with them; they will be his peoples, and God himself will be with them; he will wipe every tear from their eyes. Death will be no more; mourning and crying and pain will be no more, for the first things have passed away."*
>
> *And the one who was seated on the throne said, "See, I am making all things new."* (Revelation 21:1–5)

Amen! And Amen! Let it be so!

CHAPTER 4

BELIEVING IN GOD

The majority of Americans believe in God. Every study I have seen confirms this. In an April 26, 2018 PEW Research Center study, a robust 80% of Americans said they believe in God. Of this 80%, 70% affirmed belief in the God of the Bible, while 30% said they believed in a higher power.[1] With this affirmation as a backdrop, questions of believability in God present different issues from believability in the Bible and Jesus.

An obvious explanation for this is that what people believe about God is not necessarily related to the God they find revealed in the Bible. Simply put, one need not believe in the God of the Bible to believe in God in a larger sense. Still, much of what our American culture believes and teaches about God is rooted in images and beliefs about the God we find presented in the Bible. And generally, when we have problems with God, it is because God has been reflected to us through the language and understanding of biblical literalism, both in the reading of the biblical texts and in our teaching and language about Christian faith.

However, when we read the Bible as metaphorical narrative, a whole different meaning unfolds. It is important to note that the language we use to talk about God in the Bible is always metaphorical language. To be sure, because the nature and reality of God is always *more* than our ability to label God with words,

---

[1]PEW Research Center study, April 26, 2018.

the only language we have for conversation about God is the language of metaphor. In other words, it is not possible for us to be more definite or precise because, finally, God cannot be reduced to our verbal assessments about God.

We share metaphors verbally through language. The language of metaphorical narrative is the best we can do. However, this is not a bad thing; quite the contrary. Indeed, metaphorical language about God is not only more adequate language (meaning it comes closer to the truth of our intuitions and thoughts about God) than the language of biblical literalism, but it is also a much richer, more expansive, creative, and open way of talking about the Holy One.

Questions of believability about God are very personal. Understandably, belief or unbelief in God varies from person to person. There is a radical freedom to our belief in God. This has to be the case. Regarding questions of the Spirit, we as humans have to be free to make our own discernments. There is no other genuine way of doing faith than to do it in freedom, as we are moved by the Spirit. With this in mind, what about agnostics and atheists?

AGNOSTICS AND ATHEISTS

Above all, the idea of belief or unbelief is utterly personal. It has to be this way because anything less would lack integrity. Belief cannot be forced. It must unfold in absolute freedom. Freedom, however, has a relational context (more on this ahead), which makes it even more important in the process of believing or not believing.

In the church, we hear all the time about agnosticism and atheism with regard to God. Each is its own unique contrast to belief in God. Agnosticism holds that we cannot, in any final sense, *know* God. God is beyond our capacity to know in the way we might say we know the sun will rise tomorrow.

Certainly agnosticism introduces an element of doubt about belief in God. However, I have always considered this a positive contribution to the larger claim of belief in God. Healthy belief always includes some element of doubt, otherwise it would not be belief but something closer to a rigid, factual accounting of things (something that can be proven). Beliefs about God and faith are not airtight proofs. They are affirmations of the human mind and spirit in relation to God.

Atheism is a different perspective. It denies any belief in God. Indeed, it claims that God does not exist. However, it must be said: there are demands on atheism. Atheism must make some claim for itself; it must reveal that it has seriously considered the claims of belief. I've always liked Marcus Borg's reply when in conversation with a person claiming not to believe in God: "Tell me about the God you don't believe in."[2]

Both agnosticism and atheism are faith perspectives. They suggest belief in something, one way or another. Whatever atheists believe in—philosophy, psychology, modern science, logic, or reason—they believe in something and they view it as distinct from God.

As a church person and a person who seeks to be a Christian, I have always assumed the best about atheists and agnostics. I assume they are persons of integrity and character, as much interested in truth and love as I am. With this in mind, the church, at its best, ought to be a place where both agnostics and atheists feel welcome as they, like any of us seeking to evolve in our life journey, seek to work out the deeper meaning and purpose of their lives.

THE NAMES OF GOD

Within the tradition of Christian faith and the Bible, the names of God are many. In the New Revised Standard Version of the Bible (the Bible I use), God is known mostly by the names God, Lord, Almighty, and Father. Additional names for God that appear in other translations of the Bible are El Shaddai, Adonai, Elohim, Yahweh, and Jehovah. In our popular church talk, beyond the names God, Lord, Almighty, and Father, God is sometimes referred to as Mother, Redeemer, and Creator (i.e., Mother God, Redeemer God, Creator God).

---

[2]Marcus J. Borg, *Jesus: Uncovering the Life, Teachings, and Relevance of a Religious Revolutionary*, HarperSanFrancisco, 2006, 112.

There is another, more elusive and mysterious name for God, noted only once in Exodus 3: the reference to God as I AM, or I AM WHO I AM. This naming of God is God's reply to Moses' question of God, noted earlier:

> "*If I come to the Israelites and say to them, 'The God of your ancestors has sent me to you,' and they ask me, 'What is his name?' what shall I say to them?" God said to Moses, "I AM WHO I AM." He said further, "Thus you shall say to the Israelites, 'I AM has sent me to you.'"* (Exodus 3:13–14)

The author of John's gospel seems to have this name for God in mind when he has Jesus identify himself with the numerous I AM claims we find in John: "I am the bread of life" (6:35), "I am the light of the world" (8:12), "I am the good shepherd" (10:11), "I am the resurrection and the life" (11:25, 26), and so forth.

This naming of God in Exodus 3 is significant because it reinforces the fundamental elusiveness and mystery of God with regard to definition. God is who God is and God is always *more* than our efforts to define or label God.

Within progressive Christianity, we try to use names of God that are inclusive. For example, rather than refer to God as Father, we might refer to God as both Father and Mother. Whereas the term *Lord* (meaning "Master") is commonly used for God in the Bible, it is also used in reference to Jesus. As I noted earlier, the term *Lord* makes me uncomfortable because of the overlapping use of *Lord* to include not just God but Jesus as well. I do not believe Jesus is God, and I think it is therefore confusing to refer to Jesus as Lord. With this in mind, I tend to *not* use the term *Lord* when referring to Jesus.

HOW DO WE THINK OF GOD?

Any conversation about the nature of God must begin from a place of great humility. No matter how keen our minds or how insightful our understandings, God is always *more* than our Herculean efforts to assess, define, measure, or evaluate in any way. Whatever we think about God, however we experience God, God is always *more*.

With God, metaphorically, we are always on our knees. Still, conversation about God can be useful to us in our own personal growth. Having said this, within the possibilities and limitations of our words, we do the best we can. Before we review some of the many images of God in the Bible, what images do we personally have of God? Put another way, how do we think of God?

In our American culture, the traditional image of God is generally the God of supernatural theism, the very personal God (an actual being) that is out there, over there, and up there, orchestrating and controlling events here on earth. This is the God of antiquity, the God of the three-tiered universe: heaven above, hell below, and the earth in between. While a majority of believers most likely envision this metaphorically, still, this is the vision they hold to. This is the God that most Christians pray to when they seek divine intervention for health concerns or personal assistance of any kind. They believe (they assume) God intervenes in these ways (more on this later, in the section on God and prayer).

For me and for many progressive Christians and seekers, such a God is *not* a God we can believe in. The God of supernatural theism is simply not adequate to our evolving experience of life, faith, and the world. I do not believe that God is a being out there somewhere or up in heaven (wherever that is). Bearing this in mind, we need more expansive terms and language for talking about God.

God as Spirit

Mostly I think of God as spirit. I also think of God as the energy of infinite love in the world and as endless mystery. Both of these qualities—the energy of love and mystery—are aspects of spirit. The spirit—including love, mystery, and more—does not have any exact location; it is everywhere and anywhere, and at the same time.

The idea/reality of spirit eludes our ability to define it. It exists but we cannot say exactly what it is. Always there is a mysterious element to God, to God as *MORE*. God is the great *MORE* of the universe: *more* than our ability to describe God; *more* than our ability to measure God; *more* than our capacity to understand God. God is always *more*. It is this *more* quality that is the locus of the mystery of God.

As applied to God, spirit is the fundamental essence of God. It is *who* God is, *what* God is, and *how* God is, all at the same time. Language about the spirit is totally metaphorical. The Spirit of God is God's vital essence in the world. It is God's presence, with all of God's extraordinary qualities, which I and countless others anthropomorphize (ascribe human features to) to a considerable extent.

In our thinking about God, it is natural to anthropomorphize in some way. The most revered qualities (indeed, the only qualities) we know are human qualities. Virtually any quality of the gods or any form of animal life is identified or known by comparison to similar qualities in ourselves. In this sense, it would be difficult *not* to anthropomorphize with respect to God.

In my thinking about God, God is personal, but again, in a metaphorical sense. It is useful to think of God as having some of the best qualities we humans have: love, kindness, generosity, forgiveness, tenderness, compassion, sensitivity, and largeness of spirit. But mostly, for me, it is helpful to think of God as spirit (again, which includes God as the energy of infinite love and as endless mystery).

God as the energy of love in the world is the healing balm of the universe. It is the energy in the world that calls our best human qualities out of us. God as mystery is a reminder always of the radical *more* of God.

So again, how do we think of God? For example, when a natural disaster or some mindless act of terrorism kills hundreds of people, does God feel? Yes! Does God grieve? Yes! Does God mourn? Yes! There is no human heartbreak or personal loss that God does not feel and for which God does not have compassion. God, the Spirit, is there (i.e., in us and with us) in our darkest hour and in our most painful moment. This is part of the meaning of the cross and of Jesus' suffering and crucifixion.

God is also with us in our times of joy and celebration. God rejoices along with us whenever love, goodness, and kindness win the day. To us humans, God is both real and understood metaphorically at the same time, which is part of the mystery and radical *more* of God.

THE NATURE OF GOD

When we think about the nature of God, immediately it prompts the question, "What is God like?" In responding to this, I once again draw upon a way of thinking known as process/relational modes of thought. This way of thinking is the brainchild of my seminary professor Bernard M. Loomer, at the Graduate Theological Union in Berkeley, California, in the midseventies. Central to process and relational modes of thought are the ideas of *process* and *relationality* (noted earlier in the chapter 1).

Generally, *process* means that the universe, God, and all forms of life are in process. We are not static; we are always in the process of becoming. The God of process and relational modes of thought is a dynamic God, always evolving and unfolding, never static and unchanging. When applied to God and the Bible, this helps explain how the God of the Bible has evolved over the centuries. In the days of the patriarchs and Moses, for example, God was mostly concerned with covenant. In the time of Jesus and Paul, God is understood more through acts of compassion, justice, and suffering love.

The idea of *relationality* means that, as human beings, we are literally composed of our relationships. We are the sum total of these relationships. Think about your life and how you are, indeed, a composite of your relationships, of all the people who have *put themselves in you* over the years, through their love, kindness, dedication, and commitment.

There is always *more,* of course, because of our freedom. However, ontologically, our relationships are primary. Our freedom is an emergent of our relationships. God, too, is the sum and *more* of God's relationships. God's action in the world is fundamentally through these relationships. This is how God works in the world and in our personal and communal lives. Through infinite love and mystery, God (the Spirit) works through human beings and other forms of life.

God as Free and Relational

Because God is fundamentally relational, there is no human being or form of life with whom God is not in relationship. And because God's freedom flows out of God's relationships, God's love and energy in the world are never abstract from these relationships (never not related to them in some way).

The mystery of God is an expression of God's freedom, a dimension of God we humans can never fathom. Or we might think we have fathomed it to a point, then suddenly there is *more*. With God, there is always *more*—more mystery, more wonder, more unknown, more to be explored, more to be discovered. It never ends. But that's part of the beauty and, therein, the meaning of it all.

Life is a process of becoming in the context of our relationships, and God—as Spirit, the energy of infinite love and endless mystery—is always nudging us forward in this process.

The Size of God

As we think about God (and later, Jesus), it is helpful that we introduce the criterion of *size*. The size of a person has a lot to say about who a person is in the context of their relationships and the world. This also has application to God.

This notion of size may be a new idea for you in this regard. (I am indebted to Professor Loomer for his extensive thinking on size.) My first exposure to the term was in an intriguing seminary course my first year, taught by Dr. Loomer, entitled Theology of Sport. It was for me a fascinating course. One of our first assignments was to consider what we would generalize about sport (or, about competition). The answer Professor Loomer was looking for, we all discovered, was size. By size, Loomer means "the amount of diversity a person can include into the unity of their being and still remain a unified self."[3]

This concept holds great possibilities of meaning for us as we learn about the personalities of the Bible and seek to understand the meaning of God and Jesus. Size is a relational attribute. Again, "the size of one's spirit is measured by the range and intensity of contrasting relations a person is able to unify into

---

[3]This quotation is from class notes in a seminary course entitled Theology of Sport, fall of 1973, The Graduate Theological Union, Berkeley, California.

an aesthetic integrity." Later, Loomer adds, "the greatest size is actualized in the process of transforming almost chaotic contrasts or even human contradictions into compatible contrasts."[4]

Once we begin to get our minds around this notion of size, it can be a useful concept as we move forward. As we will see in the pages ahead, the size of a person has much to say about the person. How big and generous a spirit does the person have? How big and inclusive a love and forgiveness? How gracious and kind a heart? Again, we are talking about the stature of a person, the person's capacity to integrate different personalities and human characteristics into the unity of his or her own self.

Growing in stature and size is seldom an easy thing. Inevitably there is an element of suffering involved. Yet it is by engaging our differences that we grow. It is by welcoming in new people with fresh ideas that our personal world is expanded and enlarged. When we are able to work our way in and through the chaos of life, when we are able to take those values and beliefs that most threaten us and turn them into contrasts (which means they can live along side of each other and grow from each other), we come closer to the kingdom of God that Jesus speaks of. More on this later.

In our thinking about God, the concept of size has particular relevance. Clearly God has great size; however, it is a size we can never fully grasp because it is forever enlarging. What does this mean? It means that God is forever including (welcoming in) new and diverse relationships, situations, and meanings into the unity of God's being as Spirit, as God and the universe continue to self-create. This is an unending process.

The way greater size is achieved in relationships has to do with the way apparent incompatibilities are turned into contrasts. Take the issue of gay rights. Two decades ago, most Americans could not reconcile the idea of gay rights as an integral (i.e., accepted) part of American culture. However, now the idea of gay rights has grown and evolved in the American spirit to where these rights

---

[4]From an article by Bernard M. Loomer entitled "The Self as Communal and Relational," December, 1976.

have been notably integrated into the larger unity of who we are as Americans. Gay rights are *contrasts* to other groups' rights; they are no longer (for the majority) incompatible.

When we think about size in the Bible, a number of stories come to mind. From the Hebrew Scriptures, I love the story of Joseph's brothers being reunited with him after years apart (Genesis 45). It's a complicated story and the feelings run deep. But grace is alive and there is a beautiful forgiveness and renewal (a starting over). It is a sacred moment that evokes tears through the power of restorative forgiveness. It is a story where the largeness of love triumphs over the sins and shortcomings of the past. In this story, Joseph exhibits great size.

In the Christian Scriptures, the parable of the prodigal son from Luke 15 sounds a similar note. Again, a big forgiveness transforms the moment as the prodigal son returns from his lostness to the outstretched arms of a welcoming father. No questions are asked. An unspoken forgiveness lifts our vision of relational possibilities. The father's welcome is an example of great size of spirit.

Freedom and Creation

In simple, metaphorical language, here is how I would explain creation. Let us start with a question: Why would God choose to create the world to begin with?

Answer: Because God was lonely and wanted companionship (relationship).

Question: Why did God create the universe and humankind with freedom?

Answer: Because God wanted meaningful relationship. Meaningful relationship involves love, and love must be freely given in order to be meaningful.

In the ongoing process of becoming, the universe and we humans are free to self-create. As this process unfolds for us, there is the burden of responsibility for the consequences of the decisions we make.

As the universe continues in the unending process of self-creation, it is forever surpassing itself in the creation process in which there is always some element of mystery. So where is God in all of this? God can imagine the possibilities of creation, for both the universe and us humans. But it is not God's nature to make decisions for us as the creation process unfolds. This is not how God works. If God did decide, we would not be free and that would be a limitation of God's love. If God loves us, we have to be free to make our own decisions.

So how does this play out in the world as we experience it? Take natural disasters: Natural disasters do not happen because God wills them to happen. Hurricanes and tornados have nothing to do with God's will. (More on God's will later.)

Natural disasters happen because the universe, in the freedom of its self-creating process, moves (or evolves) in such a way that the earth quakes, or the wind currents and the seas combine to cause a hurricane, or a convergence of different forces in nature produces a fire or a tornado, or whatever it is. God doesn't make these events happen. In a sense, they *just happen*; but they just happen as a part of the self-creation of the universe. The universe, like us humans, is free to self-create as it chooses. It is an unending process. And obviously it has its chaotic elements.

With human beings, the locus of our freedom is not our minds but our spirits (our most full and essential selves). It is in our spirits that the forces of good and evil do battle to determine what we do. And all the time we are free to choose. God (the Spirit) does what God can to intervene through other people and situations, but for the most part, God hopes we make good choices that seek the best interests of the whole, of the community and the world.

For example, suppose we are tempted to do something wrong, such as not pay the correct amount for our taxes or drink more alcohol than we know we should drink. We either do or do not do the right thing. Generally we know what the right thing is. Still, there are times when we simply do the wrong thing. These are obvious examples of good-versus-poor decision-making in the exercising of our freedom.

Sometimes our decisions are totally innocuous on the surface and yet have awful consequences, such as getting into our car at a particular time and going along a particular route where, through no fault of our own, we are mauled by a truck. If we had come along thirty seconds earlier or later, nothing would have happened. There was a total randomness to the events that led to the accident. In other words, God didn't cause it to happen; we didn't do it to ourselves. It just happened, the ill-fated convergence of events where, through no fault of our own, our car gets totaled by a truck.

Random events happen all the time in life—events that are no one's fault. They just happen through an untimely convergence of events. This is part of the freedom of the world and us humans to self-create, to do what we do to make our way through life.

"Well," you may ask, "what about God?" Where is God? God is there, doing what God can to redeem whatever can be redeemed. Always, God takes what the world sends forth and works as redemptively and lovingly as God can to make things better, to give life to the situation. Always in life there is some level of suffering involved (sometimes great suffering). It is the way of things, and God suffers along with us and the world.

What do I mean by this—that in everything there is some level of suffering involved? I mean there are lingering ambiguities in everything we do and in everything that happens in life. And to the extent that there are ambiguities, there is some degree (it may be very minimal) of human suffering. For example, when we buy or sell a house, or win in a sporting competition, or our children are awarded some wonderful college scholarship, there are always consequences. It is unavoidable.

In the purchase or sale of a house, there is always something that could have gone better or worse (e.g., the price, the condition of the house, the mortgage, selling agreement). In a sports game or event, losing always hurts and winning is never perfect. There is always something that could have gone better (however small) or worse. It is the same with winning a scholarship or reaping the rewards of a great investment. There is always something that could have produced a better or worse result. There are no unambiguous events or happenings in life. Some amount of suffering (however miniscule) is always a part of things. And, of course, there are all kinds of events and happenings (i.e., personal setbacks, health issues, and tragedies) that bring about great suffering.

With regard to God's nature, God does *not* will evil or suffering on any human being or in any situation. That would be totally contrary to God's nature. God always wills the good, in all situations, for every human being and life situation. Sometimes this isn't very satisfying for us humans because, in some situations, there are not many good outcomes (e.g., war, natural disasters, human-on-human violence, etc.).

GOD'S WILL

For us humans to comment on God's will ought to be a humbling enterprise. No matter how we break it down, we can never know God's will. We can seek to discern it; we can try to understand it. Certainly we can talk about it, discuss it, conduct polls about it, and try to live it to the best of our capabilities. However, to reiterate, we can never know God's will.

In agonizing over God's will, the best we can do is a threefold process:

1. Do our best to discern God's will.

2. Hope that our actions and words reflect God's will to the greatest extent possible.

3. Get on our knees before God, in humble recognition that we can never know God's will, and ask that God's grace might bring us renewal and enlightenment.

There are two keys here: First, we need to make an effort, that is, do the very best we can to make good choices. Second, we need to display heartfelt humbleness of spirit about whatever results are forthcoming.

Some guiding questions might be helpful in the process—for example, with regard to our intended action (which we hope bends toward reflecting God's will):

1. Does it serve love's purposes?

2. Does it makes things better? Does it make the home, the workplace, the church, the community, and the world a better place?

When we talk about "love's purposes," what do we mean? To begin with, the love I am alluding to is a big love, a love of size (as I described size earlier). Love's purposes are always to make the *whole* better—the whole family, the whole team, the whole workplace, the whole church, the whole community, the whole nation, and the whole planet. The assumption is, because we are fundamentally relational creatures, when the interests and needs of *the whole* are met, the interests and needs of the individual are met as well.

In other words, when the larger needs of a family are realized, the needs of the individual family members are generally realized at the same time. On a more macro scale, the United States is strongest and most secure when rest of the international world is also relatively strong and secure. Again, we live in a relational world and universe.

GOD AND PRAYER

Prayer Is Personal

For me, prayer is very personal and is sacred activity. It is an effort to reach out to God and to the Spirit. The most genuine act of prayer *is* religious experience; it is an effort to be engaged by the grace of the Holy One. At its most sacred, prayer is greater than any words we might express in an effort to capture the yearning of our hearts and spirits. No matter how eloquent our language of prayer, the words always fall short.

Still, we use the symbols of language because we must. The mystery and deep feelings about prayer draw us in. There is relentless yearning in the spirit of us humans to embrace the divine, to feel we are walking with *God*, basking in God's love, being thankful for God's mercy and forgiveness. Again, prayer in its purest form is so very personal.

The Problem of Public Prayer in American Culture

Too often, public prayer in our culture seems contrived, even *put on*. The lofty words seem to come too easily. Many times, our public prayers seem mechanical and not from the heart. This is the challenge of praying in public settings. Still, public praying has its place if we are able to create the right mood and find the right language for the occasion. It remains forever a challenge.

To Whom Do You Pray?

To whom you pray is personal; it is subjective and personal. Having said that, I pray to God or the Spirit. I do *not* pray to Jesus. I do not pray to Jesus because I do not believe Jesus is God. This is not meant to diminish Jesus but rather to rightly exalt God. God is the one I want to pray to. More on this in the chapter on Jesus.

Does God Answer Prayer?

For me, this is complicated. However, my answer is unequivocally YES. God answers prayer. How does this happen?

It happens through the Spirit, through people, and through love. The Spirit is the essence and mystery of God and more. This Spirit (God) is everywhere. There is no place the Spirit is not. This Spirit (God) works in and through people; and it works in and through people through the energy of love. Love is the energy of God (and the Spirit) that transforms the heart, reassures the spirit, and ignites hope.

When people who are infused with love and passionate about God reach out to other human beings, or to causes or noble purposes, it makes a difference. The recipient of the prayer (when it is some noble cause, this means the leaders and most passionate supporters of the cause) cannot help but be uplifted and renewed by this love. On a feeling level (and in terms of energy), it makes a difference. Often, it brings about some level of healing and renewal.

On a bodily level, we human beings respond to love and to the Spirit (which includes the energy of love and other energy we cannot name). We cannot measure the healing or renewal, but often we can feel it. It is in this sense that prayer, indeed, makes a difference.

What Happens in Prayer?

My guess is that most people, when they pray, are praying to the God of supernatural theism; that is, the God *out there* who is looking over the world and who, when moved, will intervene in our lives in response to our most ardent prayers. Again, there are huge problems with this way of thinking about God and prayer.

Why, for instance, would a God of love bring healing to one situation and not to another? Why would a God of justice bring good fortune into the life of one needy family and not all families in need? There are no good answers to these concerns. This is another reason why we need to change the way we think about God. The God of supernatural theism is simply *not* worthy of our belief. I sometimes ask myself: How many thousands of people are there across the planet who think this is the only God they can believe in?

Yet when we think about God more as a panentheistic God, a God who is both immanent and transcendent, a God who, as energy and Spirit—as infinite love and mystery—is anywhere and everywhere, both in us and about us, and always in a process of becoming, suddenly the idea and reality of God comes alive for us.

I think that whatever happens when we pray, *happens mostly to us.* For example, when we pray for a loved one with cancer, what happens through our prayer happens mostly to us. Assuming we are sincere, we are the one mostly affected. When we pray for a loved one (or anyone), through our compassion, feelings, and love we enter into the life of their suffering and struggle, their human situation. This is the critical factor.

If we think about it, this is a powerful reality. We are not just uttering the words of prayer; we are actually, in a metaphorical way—with all the feeling and compassion we can muster—entering into the other person's suffering, deprivation, or whatever it is. It is a deeply relational experience. It takes love, energy, focus, and concentration. There is an intentionality to such prayer. There is a total giving of our deeper selves to this process.

These feelings of ours and of other persons in relation to the person for whom we are praying make a difference. When we visit this person, for example—this person for whom we have been praying—the person can feel the difference. In the process, the spirit of the situation is tangibly affected. Prayers bring healing to people because the energy of love has healing power. Simply put, always, love makes a difference.

GOD AND EVIL

In the universe and in the real world, in the human spirit and in God's Spirit, good and evil live along side of each other. For us humans, the locus of evil (as with good) is the human spirit.

As the great American theologian Reinhold Niebuhr pointed out again and again in his writings: any advance in the good entails the possibility of greater evil. (This is also called the ambiguity of "the good.") The most obvious example of this is in the world of science, particularly in the field of nuclear energy. Our learning about nuclear energy, which has many positive applications, is also the basis for almost unimaginable destruction as seen in the nuclear bomb.

So what about God and evil? God does not *do* evil; it is contrary to God's nature to work against the impulses for life. However, evil exists along with the good in the larger Spirit of God. Put another way, God lives in the midst of the evil (the darkness and woundedness) of life, just as God lives in the heartbeat of the good. Good and evil, meshed together, are part of the same reality that is the human condition (part *well-being* and part *wounded*). You cannot separate out one without affecting the other.

As an example, oftentimes a person of high energy and charisma is found to be very appealing and popular with people. However, during difficult moments and in testy situations, this same high energy and spiritedness can cause the person to overreact and to say and do things that are unbecoming. Still, if you were to take these spirited qualities out of the person, he or she may be less likely to overreact and express problematic behaviors but they would also *not* be the same person people found so engaging and fun to be around in the first place. Again, the good and the bad—together—are part of the larger reality that is the spirit of the person.

Why All the Suffering?

Why doesn't God intervene and stop evil from happening? At the prospect of a natural disaster or an unspeakable act of violence resulting in the horrible death and suffering of multitudes of people (certainly the Holocaust comes to mind), why doesn't God do something? In other words, *why all the suffering?*

Remember, the reality of God I am advocating is notably *not* the God of supernatural theism who intervenes in the world at God's own choosing. There are enormous problems with belief in such a God. For example, if God intervenes in one situation, why not in every situation of possible human suffering? Why would a loving God rescue one situation and not another? Could a God of such whim and capriciousness be worthy of our allegiance?

I do not believe it is God's nature to intervene in the natural unfolding of the creation process—not with nature (natural disasters) and not with human beings, as in war and other acts of violence. Again, God is fundamentally a relational God (and *more*). God is a composite (and *more*) of all God's relationships. God can and does work through these relationships to achieve God's purposes. But this can be messy and complicated. We human beings do not always agree on what is evil and what is not. Even when there is relative agreement, we do not always act. God can only do what we humans open ourselves to God to do (i.e., allow God to do).

Having said this, in the face and aftermath of evil, what does God do? In the wake of the devastation and suffering of war, senseless acts of violence, infant mortality, suicide, terminal diseases of all sorts, random tragedies of whatever kind, where is God?

The only answer I know is that God is there in the midst of it all—suffering, grieving, loving, showing compassion—doing whatever God can to bring healing, redemption, and new life to the situation and circumstances. Imagine the burden on a loving God in all of this! Perhaps the most vivid example—certainly for Christians—is the resurrection. After Jesus' crucifixion, which cast an awful darkness over Jesus' followers, God had another word: *This is not the end of Jesus of Nazareth but rather a new beginning.* And in the weeks, months, and perhaps even years ahead, as the reality of the Easter experience came over these early followers of Jesus, a new day was born.

Looking back at the unspeakable darkness and horror of the crucifixion, we ask, "where was God?" From the vantage point of the resurrection (which points, over time, to the birth of a new awareness and a new consciousness), we say: God was there, working through the horror, influencing events as best God could as they moved inexorably toward the birth of the resurrection experience.

The God of infinite love and compassion is forever working in the midst of whatever evil, darkness, suffering, and death come our way, seeking to give new life and new hope. God's response of compassion and love to the evil and darkness in the world is a process without end.

Why Do Bad Things Happen to Good People?

People continue to ask this question all the time. Part of the context underlying this question is the contrast, alluded to above in the section on wisdom teachings, between *conventional* wisdom and *alternative* wisdom.

In the conventional wisdom of the church and American culture, when bad things happen to people, there is some sense that it must be for something they did. In other words, the person must bear some responsibility (as insinuated by Job's friends). We see this all the time in contemporary American culture where, often, one of our political parties, for example, seeks to blame the poor for their destitution and plight. Rather than respond to the poor with compassion and generosity, they respond with the finger-pointing of guilt and irresponsibility.

Contrasted to this is the alternative wisdom of Jesus, many of the prophets, books such as Job and Ecclesiastes, and hopefully the progressive church. In this version of wisdom, when things happen to people, our first reaction is *not* some accusatory pointing of the finger but rather compassion, understanding, kindness, and love. The truth is, oftentimes there is no good explanation for why things happen. They just happen. The key is *how* we respond. This is my response (and in my view, the biblical response) to the question of bad things happening to good people. There is no good answer. Sometimes cancers appear in our bodies without any good reason. We did not deserve them; they just happened.

Again, God does what God can (through the Spirit and human touch) to mitigate the suffering and to bring wholeness and well-being. The Spirit is a powerful force for healing in the world. Still, things do not always go the way we would want them to go.

The matter of human suffering is the deepest conundrum and problem in our human situation. This would certainly be true also for God. No matter how we approach it, there are no easy answers; certainly, in many instances, no sufficiently satisfying answers. As humans we long to feel more in control (less vulnerable) in the face of the chaos and suffering that surround us. Through science, education, research, and greater acts of compassion and love, we do what we can do and simply hope for the best.

THE CHARACTER OF GOD

We see the character of God abundantly revealed in God's zeal and passion for social justice. In Israel's primal narrative of the Exodus, God stands against Pharaoh and the domination system of Egypt. In a sustained effort to liberate the suffering Israelites, God sends Moses to Egypt with explicit instructions to say to Pharaoh:

Thus says the Lord, *the God of Israel, "Let my people go, so that they may celebrate a festival to me in the wilderness."* (Exodus 5:1)

Eventually, in the Exodus experience, the Israelites are freed from lives of economic exploitation and political oppression in Egypt. God has seen Israel's misery and suffering, and through Moses God has acted. In Israel's unfolding history, she would forever remember God's liberating action on her behalf. Again and again over the centuries, in an effort to encourage her and inspire her, the prophets of Israel would remind her of the Exodus experience and of God's rescuing her from slavery in Egypt.

A few centuries later, when Israel became a monarchy (first under King Saul, followed soon by King David and King Solomon and, finally, the era of the divided kingdom), invariably the kings and the elites would regress to a period of neglect and exploitation of the poor. In response, God would send forth prophet after prophet to announce God's protest. God's passion for social justice never abated. Again, God's preferential option for the poor was a reminder of God's character and of who God is as the holy God of Israel.

In our modern world, God's passion for social justice burns on. As circumstances permit, God is forever working through people and situations to bring about a more just and fair world. In recent times we see this in the significant progress we have made in the areas of race relations (although recent events remind us we still have a long way to go with this one), gender equality and, particularly, in the human rights of gays and lesbians.

These reforms all take place over time, of course, as part of an ongoing process. There is always more that God would have us do, always more that needs to be achieved. Perhaps the most alarming concern recently is the glaring, widening income gap between the rich and the poor. Other areas where reforms are needed are gun control, immigration, global warming and the environment, education, campaign finance, and voter suppression. Always, the Spirit of God and the justice of God work together to usher in a better day.

Let us look now to some of the images of God in the Bible.

IMAGES OF GOD IN THE HEBREW SCRIPTURES

The considerable array of images of God in the Bible help give us a glimpse (from the Bible's point of view) of who God is and what God is like. We should remember that images are always abstractions; they are partial glimpses into the reality of God. Still, they are useful in giving us handles for thinking about God and understanding God. We should take note how the images of God have evolved over the centuries. First, from the Hebrew Bible.

The Image of God in Creation

The evocative creation stories of the Hebrew Bible are rich, metaphorical narrative. In six days the Creator God calls the world into being then pauses to rest on the seventh day (the Sabbath). The stories reveal an authoritative image of God that would be nonsensical to take literally. The biblical language of creation is the author's best effort to explain the mystery of creation within the language and myth of the ancient world.

The Image of God in the Covenants

Another prominent image of God in the Hebrew Bible is the image of God in the covenants. A covenant is like a spiritual arrangement or agreement. In the arrangement, God agrees to love, guide, and protect Israel, while Israel agrees to honor the covenants with God with her obedience.

God makes a covenant with Abraham and Sarah of which circumcision is the sign of the covenant. Later, God makes a covenant with Moses at Mount Sinai in the giving of the commandments. Still later, God calls forth prophet after prophet to remind Israel of the imperative of covenantal obedience.

As the years unfold, Israel falters badly, and eventually both the northern kingdom of Israel (722 BCE) and the southern kingdom of Judah (587 BCE) are destroyed (by Assyria and Babylon, respectively). Finally, centuries later, God forms a covenant through Jesus of Nazareth, symbolized by the breaking of the bread and the sharing of the cup in the Lord's Supper. These stories of covenant are all metaphorical narratives serving to remind Israel of who she is in relation to God.

The Image of God in the Exodus

The image of God in the Exodus is one of great compassion and power. Here we see vivid displays of God's passion for social justice. God has heard Israel's cries of suffering. The God of the Exodus is a God who stands in protest against the domination systems of the world (in this case, Egypt). God's rescuing the Israelites through Moses is a metaphorical narrative depicting God's compassion for human suffering and abiding commitment to social and economic justice.

The Image of the God of Israel as a Jealous God

In the first of the Ten Commandments there is an image of God as a *jealous* God:

> *I am the* Lord *your God, who brought you out of the land of Egypt, out of the house of slavery; you shall have no other gods before me.* (Exodus 20:2–3)

Later in Deuteronomy, in what is known as the Shema, there is further emphasis of this theme:

> *Hear, O Israel: The* Lord *is our God, the* Lord *alone. You shall love the* Lord *your God with all your heart, and with all your soul, and with all your might.* (Deuteronomy 6:4–5)

The idea of God being a jealous God actually plays out as God being intolerant of rival gods (a prominent theme in the Hebrew Bible). This is all metaphorical, of course; but God's anger is most roused when Israel forgets the covenants and slips into idol worship of any kind. The wisdom of the Bible suggests that the fear of the Lord is the beginning of wisdom. *Fear* here is comparable to a deep awe and respect of the kind that would never do anything to make God jealous. Such behavior would simply be outside the boundaries of something one would do.

As we can see, the images of God in the Hebrew Scriptures are diverse and extensive. The Psalms overflow with a splendid array of images of God, some of which were revealed in the discussion of the Bible as sacred and sacramental, early in chapter 3; and others, in the more lengthy discussion of Psalms in the Wisdom teaching of chapter 3.

The final two images I want to touch on as biblical images of God in the Hebrew Scriptures are the images of God as a God of hope and as a God of suffering love.

The God of Hope

The image of God as the God of hope is a compelling and uplifting theme in the Bible. Sometimes hope is all we have as we face the tough challenges life sends our way. Check out these words of hope from the prophet of the Exile, Second Isaiah! As you will recall, the prophet is speaking to Israel in Babylonian exile. Israel has been mired in exile for almost fifty years. She is desperate for a flickering light of hope for a better day:

> *Have you not known? Have you not heard? The LORD is the everlasting God, the Creator of the ends of the earth. He does not faint or grow weary; his understanding is unsearchable. . . . But those who wait for the LORD shall renew their strength, they shall mount up with wings like eagles, they shall run and not be weary, they shall walk and not grow faint.* (Isaiah 40:28, 31)

The image of God here is of a God of resilience and steadfastness. Isaiah is reminding Israel that her God is *the* very Creator God that called the world into being; her God is not some fly-by-night God who cannot be counted on. Israel need only be strong in her hope and patient in the passion of her resolve.

The God of Suffering Love

The image of God as the God of suffering love, from the fourth servant song of Isaiah 53, helps us glimpse the way of God's redemptive purposes. Suffering love is the best way God knows for personal and communal transformation:

> *Who has believed what we have heard? And to whom has the arm of the Lord been revealed? . . . But he was wounded for our transgressions, crushed for our iniquities; upon him was the punishment that made us whole, and by his bruises, we are healed.* (Isaiah 53:1, 5)

As we continue to highlight biblical images of God, let us now turn to images of God we find in the Christian Scriptures. Again, these images help paint a picture for us of who God is and what God is like.

IMAGES OF GOD IN THE CHRISTIAN SCRIPTURES

The God of Compassion

One of the core images of God in the Christian Bible is the image of God as a God of compassion. Compassion is fundamentally central to who God is and what God is like. God's deep compassion is the moral basis for God's deep passion for social and economic justice. Throughout the Bible, God reveals a clear preferential option for the poor. In Luke 6:36, the author of Luke has Jesus say: "Be compassionate as God is compassionate."

This translation differs in some Bibles but is the preferred translation for our purposes here. We find this core image of God abundantly revealed in Jesus. Indeed, it is a central part of who Jesus is (more on this in the chapter on Jesus).

The God of Love

When reflecting on the Christian faith, I like to say, "It's all about the love." Again and again, this is where our faith leads us. Every day, as the sun sets in the west and as we look back at our day and our lives, it is all about the love. The image of *God* as love runs through the Christian Scriptures:

> *Beloved, let us love one another, because love is from God; everyone who loves is born of God and knows God. Whoever does not love does not know God, for God is love.*
>
> *God is love, and those who abide in love abide in God, and God abides in them.* (1 John 4:7–8, 16b)

At the conclusion of Romans 8, in one of Paul's most well-known affirmations of God, he talks about how nothing can separate us from Christ's love:

> *Neither death, nor life, nor angels, nor rulers, nor things present, nor things to come, nor powers, nor height, nor depth, nor anything else in all creation, will be able to separate us from the love of God in Christ Jesus our Lord.* (Romans 8:38–39)

The God of Suffering Love

The God of suffering love is so important in the Bible that we point to it in both the Hebrew and Christian Scriptures. In the Christian Scriptures the image of God as the God of suffering love is embodied in Paul's proclamation of Christ crucified. Suffering love is the primary value of God and, by relationship, of Jesus. It is *the* love that offers the greatest hope for redeeming the world and for creating a world of greater peace with justice. Suffering love creates in all of us a way of personal transformation. However, it is a way of personal transformation that leads to community transformation as well.

The image of Christ crucified would seem to present a contradiction. About this, Paul says:

> *Has not God made foolish the wisdom of the world? . . . For Jews demand signs and Greeks desire wisdom, but we proclaim Christ crucified, a stumbling block to Jews and foolishness to Gentiles, but to those who*

are the called, both Jews and Greeks, Christ the power of God and the wisdom of God. For God's foolishness is wiser than human wisdom, and God's weakness is stronger than human strength. (1 Corinthians 1:20b, 22–25)

Christ crucified points to the great evil committed by Roman law and Jewish Torah in the crucifixion of Jesus. But it was *this* Jesus (crucified) that God raised from the dead. (We need to read this metaphorically.) In Jesus' gift to us of his crucifixion, we are invited to embrace the way of suffering love that God claimed (in Jesus' resurrection) as God's way as well.

GOD AND SALVATION

Salvation is a loaded idea in our Christian faith. Within traditional, conservative-evangelical Christianity, it is a popular topic of conversation and concern. Indeed, evangelicals are fascinated with salvation. In common conversation with evangelicals, how often do we hear the simplistic question come up, "Are you saved?"

Beyond being annoying, the question is more than a little presumptuous. It assumes that a person can actually *know*, definitively, about their salvation. Sometimes I want to say, "Whoa, slow down a bit, people. Who is it who does the saving? Is it not God? How then can we possibly know anything about who is saved or not saved? And is it not, indeed, more than a little presumptuous to think that we do?" Always, in every instance, whatever salvation is, it is God's domain.

Curiously enough, the Jesus of the gospels was not much concerned about salvation, nor was Jesus much concerned about the afterlife. His only comments on salvation were in response to questions put to him in Matthew's story of the rich young man, when Jesus tells his disciples:

"Truly I tell you, it will be hard for a rich person to enter the kingdom of heaven. Again I tell you, it is easier for a camel to go through the eye of a needle than for someone who is rich to enter the kingdom of God." (Matthew 19:23–24)

Hearing this, the disciples were clearly dismayed and asked, "Then who can be saved?" Jesus answers them, saying, "For mortals it is impossible, but for God all things are possible" (Matthew 19:25–26). What God and Jesus *are* concerned about are people living lives of personal transformation and social responsibility.

For progressive Christians in the emerging church, the emphasis is not on who's in or who's out in some poorly conceived salvation paradigm. The emphasis is on lives of transformation, both for the individual and the community.

IS THE BIBLE THE WORD OF GOD?

Earlier we noted that the Bible is not of divine origin. Indeed, over a period of some eleven hundred years, the Bible was written by human beings. This is not to suggest that these human persons were *not* inspired by God and the Spirit. Obviously they were.

For biblical literalists—those who claim inerrancy and infallibility for the Bible—the argument would be that the Holy Spirit inspired the biblical writers (editors, too) in some manner that was beyond any possibility for error or falsehood. This is such a weak argument, one hardly knows where to begin. A person would have to pretty much suspend any logical or reasonable method of judgment to sustain such a belief.

In our churches, all the time, we matter-of-factly refer to the Bible as "the Word of God." Ironically, if taken literally, the Bible is not *the Word of God*. However, in a metaphorical sense, the Bible is an emergent of the divine-human relationship. While humans wrote the Bible, these humans were no doubt people of faith who were in a constant process of discernment (with God and the Spirit) about the meaning and truth of what they were writing. In this larger sense, the Bible is very much related to God and to God's purposes.

To state this again, while the Bible is *not* a divine product, it is the product of the divine-human relationship. It is an expression of the purposes of God as these purposes are revealed in and through God's relationship with the biblical authors.

In our contemporary worship, therefore, after reading from the scriptures, we would be better served by saying not "the Word of the Lord, or the Word of God" but rather something like "Hear now what the Spirit is saying to the church."[5] (Language like this was suggested by Marcus J. Borg some years back.)

---

[5] The New Zealand Book of Common Prayer.

CHAPTER 5

THE JESUS YOU DIDN'T KNOW
YOU COULD BELIEVE IN

More than thirty years ago, in a book titled *Love in the Ruins*, Walker Percy wrote, "We live in a Christ-forgetting and Christ-haunted death-dealing Western world. . . ."[1]

And to be sure, just as there is much we do not remember about Jesus—particularly when it's not to our convenience or in our perceived best interests—still, we remain fascinated with him.

Think back to 2004. Remember all the curiosity and conversation around Mel Gibson's *The Passion of Christ*? For a period of months, commentary on this movie dominated our American culture. It was a movie that did not allow us to remain indifferent. It engaged us and made us think and reflect; it challenged us to make personal decisions around questions of faith.

Not long after that, in the same year, the book *The DaVinci Code* came out and became an immediate best seller. It was a story revolving around Jesus and the very real possibility that he had intimate relations with Mary Magdalene. Again, as a culture we remain fascinated with Jesus. What to think about him and believe about him? And for Christians, how to follow him and be his faithful disciples?

---

[1]Marcus J. Borg, *Jesus: Uncovering the Life, Teachings, and Relevance of a Religious Revolutionary*, page 3, quotation from *Love in the Ruins*, by Walker Percy, HarperSanFrancisco.

SOURCES ON JESUS

For the most well-known human being in the history of the planet, it may seem strange that we have only two sources for information about the historical Jesus. One source, from the Jewish historian Josephus, writing perhaps a decade before the end of the first decade CE, offers only scant information. Still, it remains the only non-Christian source we have. The other source, of course, is the Bible—namely, the four gospels. Although we have obvious references to Jesus in Paul's letters and in the noncanonical gospels (e.g., the Gospel of Thomas), none of these other sources provides new information on Jesus' life.

In his history of the Jewish revolt against Rome in 66 CE, a revolt resulting in a crushing defeat at the hands of the forces of empire, Josephus offers the following reference to Jesus:

> At this time there appeared Jesus, a wise man. . . . For he was a doer of startling deeds, a teacher of people who received the truth with pleasure. And he gained a following both among many Jews and among many of Greek [meaning "Gentile," that is, non-Jewish] origin. . . . And when Pilate, because of an accusation made by the leading men among us, condemned him to the cross, those who had loved him previously did not cease to do so. . . . And up until this very day, the tribe of Christians, named after him, has not died out.[2]

Most people in the United States and in the Western world believe something about Jesus. However, *what* we believe and *how* we practice what we believe involve a tremendous range. For the majority (that has been in decline for decades), Jesus is viewed as some combination of personal Savior, Son of God, risen Lord, living Christ, lamb of God, God's Messiah, light of the world, good shepherd, and founder of the Christian faith. Still, for countless others, views on Jesus vary widely—from being considered a very good and admirable man to wonderment about whether he actually lived at all.

---

[2]Flavius Josephus, *Jewish Antiquities*, 18:63–64.

For those increasingly on the margins of the church and on the outside, some general, emerging observations about belief in Jesus:

- For many, mostly the young and more educated, the way Jesus is presented in the institutional church is problematic and increasingly *not* believable. Some of these same people view Jesus as an admirable human being but cannot relate to the additional layers of belief (e.g., he is divine, performed miracles, died for our sins, etc.) that are attached to him.

- The Jesus of the gospels (our overwhelmingly primary source on Jesus), where the gospels are understood to be *literally* true and factual, is increasingly viewed as fanciful and *not* believable.

- Related to the above, belief in Jesus as God (as fully divine) and as personal Savior who died for our sins is increasingly problematic. For many persons, this way of believing doesn't make sufficient sense and suggests what I can only call bad theology and Christology (way of thinking about God and Jesus).

Specific traditionally held beliefs about Jesus that these *many* people either do not believe or find increasingly problematic are:

- That Jesus was born of a virgin. Most modern people, with hefty support from the majority of modern biblical scholars, do not believe in the virgin birth. They believe Jesus had a biological mother and father (most likely, Mary, and perhaps Joseph), just like the rest of us.

- That Jesus actually *did* all the miracles attributed to him, such as walk on water, turn water into wine, and raise people from the dead. Generally, these people do *not* believe Jesus actually did these things.

- That Jesus will literally come again (i.e., the Second Coming). This group of people finds traditional belief in the Second Coming simply not credible.

LITERALISM AND BELIEF IN JESUS

In seeking to understand what all of this means for the church and for what those of us in progressive Christian circles call the emerging church, it is helpful to point out that virtually all of the above-noted problems and stumbling blocks are rooted in (can be explained by) a literal reading of the Bible.

As noted earlier, biblical literalism, which means understanding the Bible as the infallible, inerrant Word of God, is *the* major divide in the church in this second decade of the twenty-first century. This point cannot be made too strongly. Taking the Bible literally teaches that the events described in the Bible (e.g., the creation stories and details of the Exodus story, along with Jesus' alleged deeds and miracles) actually happened; that they are historically factual. More still, their historical happening is viewed as critical to belief, which suggests that if these events did not actually happen, the foundation of Christian belief would be irretrievably shattered.

Curiously enough, biblical literalism—reflecting a personal choice about how to read the Bible—is a relatively recent phenomenon. Christian fundamentalism, out of which this emphasis on a literal reading of the scriptures evolved, is a late-nineteenth-century–early-twentieth-century phenomenon. Historically, it is a relatively recent development.

Prior to the emergence of fundamentalism in the church and in the way Christian faith came to be presented, a more or less undeclared *natural literalism* prevailed within Christianity. People simply understood the Bible (and later, after the invention of the printing press in the 1400s, *read* the Bible) as literally true in a natural manner. This sort of natural literalism was taken for granted. It was the way things were. There was no reason for debate or argument.

In the aftermath of the Enlightenment (seventeenth and eighteenth centuries) and with the advent of modern science, gradually this natural literalism gave way (particularly in the United States) to a more *conscious literalism*. Whereas natural literalism did not involve a decision of the will about how to read the Bible (it was simply the way that was passed on through the centuries), conscious literalism involved a willful decision about how the scriptures should be read.

The problem of biblical literalism has existed for countless decades within the church. However, in recent decades and into the present, its implications for

Christian belief and church participation are causing increasing numbers of people to debunk the church and turn away from the Christian faith.

Most of these persons believe in God, either believe in Jesus or are curious about him, and would like to believe the Bible but find much of the language about both Jesus and the Bible *not* believable. Part of the problem is that even though many churches (mostly mainline Protestant), local church pastors, seminary professors, and theologians are not advocates of biblical literalism, still, the language of this literalism, passed on through the years, remains by and large the language of Christian faith.

With all of this in mind, the purpose of this chapter, "The Jesus You Didn't Know You Could Believe In," is to present Jesus in language and in ways that, while remaining faithful to the integrity of the New Testament writings, are both believable and transformative for people of faith.

TWO PERSPECTIVES OF JESUS

Before going any further, I want to state clearly that the Jesus you didn't know you could believe in was totally human to the core, just as you and I are human (more on this later). I do not believe that Jesus was God. I *do* believe that Jesus' life was centered in God and revealed significant glimpses of God, but he himself was not divine. Nor do I believe that Jesus thought of himself as divine. In the pages ahead, I want to reflect more deeply on Jesus' humanity and its importance for Christian faith. However, as background for this, it is important that we make a clear distinction between the *pre-Easter* and the *post-Easter* Jesus. Grasping the implications of this distinction is critical to our understanding of what Christian faith has been through the centuries as well as the possibilities a more enlightened Christian faith holds for the future.

The term *enlightened* is used here to suggest that our Christian faith is part of a developing tradition. This is always the case. Understandings of God, Jesus, and the Bible are never static. They are always developing, always in a process of evolving and unfolding as new understandings and insights are uncovered. To be enlightened is to be open to these new developments.

The Pre-Easter Jesus

The gospels were written some forty to seventy years after Jesus' crucifixion and resurrection. In our effort to appreciate who Jesus was as an historical person, as a human being who walked the earth just like any human person walks the earth, these forty to seventy years suggest a significant time period. Trying to get back to the historical Jesus through the eyes of the four different gospel writers is, therefore, no small task.

To begin with, given this elapsed time period, the gospels have to be considered as some combination of history remembered and metaphorical narrative. The two earliest sources of information on Jesus in the gospels are Q, written probably in the 50s CE, and Mark, generally dated around 70 CE. Both Matthew and Luke (about 80 and 85 CE) used both Mark and Q as well as their own sources. As we can see, getting back to who Jesus was as an historical person is a complicated process.

No matter how sincere our intent, most of what we know about Jesus comes to us through the post-Easter reflections of the faith communities out of which the respective gospels emerged. These different communities (evolving churches) each had their own identity and therein their own problems and concerns, along with their own hopes for their future. Having said this, what can we say about the pre-Easter Jesus?

Coming from a peasant family, Jesus was probably born in Nazareth; and his biological parents were probably Mary and Joseph (although there is some doubt about the identity of the latter). Also, from what we know, Jesus had a number of siblings. One brother, James, whom we can assume Jesus knew well, went on to become a key pillar of the mother church in Jerusalem (along with Peter and John), until his untimely death at the scandalous hands of the interim high priest, Ananus, in 62 CE.

(Although most Christians are unaware of this, the New Testament letter of James is thought to be portions of James' sermons given over the years. Assuming this to be the case—and because Jesus and James were thought to have a close relationship—it is very probable that the letter in James' name reflects some of Jesus' thinking as well.)

In trying to assess what Jesus' life was like growing up in Nazareth, if Joseph was his father and was indeed a carpenter, as the tradition suggests, it is very likely that Jesus knew something of carpentry himself. Given the parables that he told and his relationship with his disciples, he must have known something of the lives of fishermen as well as the agrarian, peasant culture that surrounded him.

However, before his death and resurrection, as the pre-Easter Jesus, what was Jesus like in his life and active ministry (a period of probably up to eighteen months, although some scholars suggest it was as long as three years)? What was he about and what was he up to? In responding to this, I want to use the five categories established by Marcus J. Borg, mostly from his book, *The Meaning of Jesus*, coauthored with N. T. Wright.

To begin with, according to Borg, the pre-Easter Jesus was a *spirit person,* or a *Jewish mystic.* He uses these terms interchangeably. Beyond this, he was also a *healer,* a *wisdom teacher,* a *social prophet,* and a *movement initiator.*

Spirit Person, or Jewish Mystic

Mystics are persons who have experiences of God. They have a sense of raised consciousness and awareness. They are people who have relatively clear (for them) experiences of the sacred. While these experiences do not lend themselves to being measured and cannot generally be described in ordinary language, still, for the mystic, they are real.

There is a certain knowing for the mystic that goes beyond the cognitive. In this sense, he or she is highly intuitive. The mystical cannot always be grasped with language, and when it can, it is virtually always the language of metaphor.

In the gospel accounts Jesus is presented as being notably God-centered. There is this palpable *God-presence* quality about him, as if God or the Spirit were somehow in him in a gripping way. In the gospels he often goes off by himself to pray or meditate (i.e., for personal time with God). Whatever else we might say about Jesus, this God presence seemed to be in him in profound and life-giving ways.

Very probably Jesus' experiences of God as a spirit person influenced everything about the way he embraced the world. His centeredness in God was always nudging him and prompting him to see the world and relationships in a particular way. Another word for the God presence that shined through Jesus is *love*—a love that urges us to turn the other cheek, love our enemies, bring good news to the poor, and let the oppressed go free.

The bottom line here is that the pre-Easter Jesus was a remarkable human being, a quality we do not want to lose in the rush of the post-Easter faith communities to attach divine qualities to Jesus. More on this later in a more in-depth consideration of Jesus as fully human.

Healer

In Mark, the earliest gospel, from the beginning of Jesus' public activity and ministry, Jesus is depicted healing people of one ailment or another. The author of Mark has him casting out demons and curing the sick of a whole range of diseases. Later, he heals paralytics, restores sight to the blind, and somehow brings the dead back to life. Supposing only some of this is historically true, we can only imagine how fast news spread of Jesus' healing powers.

Although we can never *know* to what extent Jesus was able to actually heal afflicted persons, there is no reason to doubt that some degree of what Borg calls "paranormal" healings were done by him. *Paranormal* refers to beyond the ordinary. Again, the power of Jesus' God presence, along with his love and compassion for the afflicted, would certainly make some level of healing possible.

We hear of "paranormal" healings all the time. We can't necessarily explain them, yet they do seem to happen. Given how much we still have to learn about the brain and the power of the brain to affect our physical self, who is to say to what extent paranormal healings happen? Quite possibly, in the years ahead, what we view today as paranormal might be considered normal. Looking back, we can only say that Jesus must have been an extraordinary and gifted healer.

Wisdom Teacher

At the core of wisdom teaching in the Bible is a new way of seeing God, relationships, and community life. The old way is the way of conventional wisdom, or the way we are all acculturated to think and live. We are all born into particular, socially ingrained ways of seeing all that we see in life. There is nothing inherently wrong with this. It is just that it is limited and can only take us so far in our relationship with God and the sacred.

One of Jesus' unique gifts to us, beyond his crucifixion, was the gift of his parables, which were utterly unique, insightful, probing, and enlightening. We might ask ourselves: Where did they come from? Although we can never totally account for them (i.e., no doubt some of the parables came from other sources or were creations of the gospel authors), they must have come from his unconventional wisdom as a teacher, from the unique, mystical depths of his spirit and from his centeredness in God.

Jesus taught in aphorisms and parables overflowing with metaphor. He taught from the perspective of a new way of seeing God, the sacred, and the world. It was a way enlightened and guided by a compassion and love that saw the light of God's purposes reflected in all people. It was also, of course, a way that put him in conflict with the religious leaders who were protectors of the status quo.

The unconventional wisdom of Jesus—his new way of seeing—was the way of a big love and a humble spirit. Perhaps nowhere is this more abundantly seen than in the timeless parable of the prodigal son: the unconditional love of the expectant father; where love is more powerful than pride and ego, and where forgiveness is more Godlike than obedience and conventional fairness. A new way of seeing takes us to places within the sacred that the old way can never take us. It takes us to new and deeper awareness and understanding of God.

Social Prophet

Growing up, certainly Jesus had heard about Israel's prophets and the prophetic tradition. During his lifetime and active ministry, the Law and the wisdom of the prophets would have been in manuscript form and, no doubt, would have been commonly read in the synagogues and at other religious gatherings.

It is very probable that Israel's prophets were mystics, persons who experienced God and God's passion for justice in powerful and life-deepening ways. From the time of the Exodus, the biblical prophets of Israel had spoken out against the domination systems of the earth, those structures of government and rule that sustained and enforced the huge divide between the wealthy elites and the marginalized peasant poor.

Again and again, over the centuries, prophetic voices rose up, filled with passion for God and no less passion for social justice. Oftentimes these prophets experienced visions that inspired them and fueled their prophetic impulse. Check out the vision experienced by the eighth-century prophet Isaiah in the call of Isaiah from Isaiah 6:

> In the year that King Uzziah died, I saw the Lord sitting on a throne, high and lofty; and the hem of his robe filled the temple. Seraphs were in attendance above him; each had six wings: with two they covered their faces, and with two they covered their feet, and with two they flew. And one called to another and said:
>
> "Holy, holy, holy is the LORD of hosts; the whole earth is full of his glory."
>
> The pivots on the thresholds shook at the voices of those who called, and the house filled with smoke. And I said: "Woe is me! I am lost, for I am a man of unclean lips, and I live among a people of unclean lips; yet my eyes have seen the King, the LORD of hosts!"
>
> Then one of the seraphs flew to me, holding a live coal that had been taken from the altar with a pair of tongs. The seraph touched my mouth with it and said: "Now that this has touched your lips, your guilt has departed and your sin is blotted out." Then I heard the voice of the Lord saying, "Whom shall I send, and who will go for us?" And I said, "Here am I; send me!" (Isaiah 6:1–8)

We cannot help but ask ourselves: How would a God-centered person such as Jesus, a person with immense gifts of healing and wisdom teaching—a peasant himself—not be deeply moved by such a text? Generally, for the prophets and certainly for Jesus himself, a passion for social justice burned in their spirits. In the historical context of Jesus' life situation—particularly given the God presence that was in him—Jesus was a social justice prophet not unlike the great social justice prophets of Israel before him.

Domination systems are powerful realities. As Jesus' advocacy for the poor and the marginalized continued to sound out, it was only a matter of time before the leaders of the domination system decided they had had enough of him and sought to permanently silence his voice. More on this when we look at the death and resurrection of Jesus.

Movement Initiator

The pre-Easter Jesus "became" all of these things we are saying about him. He wasn't born any of these things. These aspects of his life that we are identifying all grew within him, starting with the sense of himself as a spirit person. The God presence in Jesus must have vibrated in his spirit from early on. For example, I cannot imagine him just waking up one day and saying, "I think I'll go start a movement." My guess is that, as the Spirit moved, the movement began to rise up around him as he went about his business of being this Spirit-filled person.

No doubt the healings came first, and, of course, any such healings would have attracted a crowd. Who would not be drawn to someone with the sort of healing powers attributed to Jesus (some of which must have actually happened)? At some point, Jesus' gifts as a wisdom teacher began to naturally unfold as well. Very likely, his role as a social prophet came later, simply as a logical consequence of being all these other things.

Given all of the above activity, it is not much of a reach to imagine elements of a movement just sort of happening. The part I am curious about is the calling of his disciples. In Mark, the first gospel, about one-third into the first chapter,

Jesus calls his first disciples: the brothers Peter and Andrew, followed by the sons of Zebedee, James, and John, all of whom are fishermen. Halfway into chapter 2, he calls Levi (sometimes called Matthew, the tax collector). Finally, from a gathered crowd, near the midpoint of chapter 3, he appoints the remaining seven. He seems to orient them somewhat, then, a short time later, he sends them out in twos to cast out demons and spread the message of repentance.

The calling of the disciples, about whom we actually know very little, would seem to constitute the early stages of a movement, yet as the gospel stories unfold, their role seems to diminish. What does not diminish are the increasing numbers of followers, which would make total sense given the range of deeds and teachings attributed to Jesus. Simply put, people are drawn to Jesus. As we will emphasize still more when we look at the post-Easter Jesus, *there is something about him.* Indeed, it is this special *something* that eventually plants the seeds for the first post-Easter communities of faith.

The Post-Easter Jesus

As noted earlier, other than the brief historical reflections of the Jewish historian Josephus, the only information we have on Jesus comes to us from the four gospels, the letters of Paul, and the remaining letters and books of the Christian Scriptures.[3] These New Testament sources on Jesus are mostly post-Easter metaphorical narrative. As we have observed, some of the gospels is history remembered, but the overwhelming majority of it is metaphorical narrative (or history remembered metaphorized).

To get our minds around the meaning and the reality of the post-Easter Jesus, we have to remember again that these gospel accounts were penned forty to seventy years after the Easter experience. Remembering this helps to slow down the unfolding of events taking place in the early Christian communities and gives them a chance to take root and unfold.

---

[3]Perhaps the Gospel of Thomas should be added to this list.

When I say "Christian communities," I should note that these communities, or groups of people who were followers of the way taught by Jesus of Nazareth, were Jewish; the term *Christian* wasn't used to identify Jesus' followers until some years later. As Jesus-believing Jews, they continued to worship in the synagogues. For them, the synagogue had been the center of their lives. This didn't suddenly change in the early months and years after Jesus died. Indeed, it wasn't until around the tenth decade (around the time John's gospel was authored) that the Jewish religious leaders began to ban Jesus-believing Jews from the synagogues.

Post-Easter reflections on Jesus—on the meaning of his life, his teachings, and certainly his crucifixion—took time to evolve. When we read the New Testament, it is easy to see the Jesus story taking place in a timely, linear fashion— from the birth narratives on through his baptism, his active ministry, leading up to the events of Holy Week and the Easter experience. But again, this was not the case. These gospel accounts are largely metaphorical narrative written some forty to seventy years later.

In thinking about this, we have to ask ourselves what it must have been like being a follower of Jesus in the early weeks and months after his crucifixion. Whatever the resurrection was, it evolved out of a new energy and spirit that emerged from the ashes of Good Friday. Early on there must have been some vital sense of Jesus being a living reality among them. Although he had died a gruesome death on the cross, still, somehow his spirit (the essence of who he was as a spirit person) was alive to them.

At the core of the resurrection, of the Easter experience, is the undeniable reality that, after Jesus' resurrection (or as the experience of resurrection unfolded), his disciples and followers were all changed; they were all different. No doubt this was a gradual process over a period of months, if not years. Somehow, amazingly, they were *not* the same people they had been before his resurrection. The living reality of their changed lives is perhaps the most powerful and persuasive testimony we have of the resurrection.

I will reflect on the resurrection more later. However, for the moment, it is important that we try to understand how Jesus' followers, after his resurrection, had a very real sense of him still being with them (with them in spirit or in a way that was real for them). Again, in whatever ways, they continued to experience him as a living reality.

With this as a backdrop, as the years unfolded, these early communities of followers began to increasingly attribute qualities of God to Jesus. And when these experiences of the post-Easter Jesus were recorded, the language used was the language of metaphorical narrative. These metaphorical narratives themselves became a part of the developing tradition within the early Christian communities. The problem is that, later, after the Christian Church became almost totally Gentile, the Christian communities began to increasingly read these metaphorical narratives in a literal way.

As we can see, therefore, metaphorical narrative about Jesus—about who he was and the ways he was alive to them—became *the* language and *the* story about Jesus for the emerging church and even up to our modern period.

The Gospels and the Post-Easter Jesus

Written forty to seventy years after the resurrection, the gospels are all post-Easter memories and metaphorical narratives about Jesus. They are the historical memory and testimony—mostly, no doubt, second- or thirdhand or more—of those who knew or had heard about Jesus. Again, they are metaphorical narrative, seeking to paint a particular picture of Jesus that would be persuasive with their own communities of faith. It is important to remember that each gospel writer had his own purposes emerging out of his own particular community.

As we can see and imagine, over the years memories and images of the post-Easter Jesus evolved. This process of evolution continues in our own time. However, it is important that we remember that most of our understandings and beliefs about Jesus are rooted less in what we know of the pre-Easter Jesus and more in the language and images (the metaphorical narrative) passed down through the years of the post-Easter Jesus.

The Post-Easter Jesus Grew Out of the Community's Memory of the Pre-Easter Jesus

Given my belief in the importance of the humanity of Jesus, both to strengthen the theology of the church from within as well as to appeal to those for whom the church and Jesus have become increasingly irrelevant, this is an important statement. What this statement affirms is that the post-Easter Jesus of the early Christian communities was deeply influenced by memories people had of the pre-Easter Jesus. In other words, this pre-Easter Jesus had to have been a remarkable human being.

As a person walking the earth in first-century Palestine, Jesus had uncommon depth and appeal as a spirit person, a mystic, and also a revolutionary prophet. His healings struck amazement in people; his wisdom teaching, through cryptic sayings and brilliant parables, touched people deeply. His courage, charisma, and zeal moved people to follow him. He must have been truly, stunningly captivating.

The Post-Easter Jesus and the Living Christ

As the years marched on, the post-Easter Jesus evolved into the *living Christ*. No doubt, this was a gradual process. For me, the idea of *Christ* is a universal reality. *Christ*, coming from the Greek, *Christos*, and *Messiah* (Hebrew for "Christ") mean the "anointed one of God." I believe Jesus of Nazareth (the historical Jesus) became the living Christ on the cross, through suffering unto death. Death often brings a universal remembering about those who have died. People such as Socrates, Harriet Tubman, Mahatma Gandhi, Martin Luther King Jr., Mother Teresa, and Nelson Mandela become in death even more than they were in life.

After his crucifixion and resurrection, we can imagine believers continuing to experience visions and apparitions of Jesus, along with a very real sense that he was still with them in spirit. Early on, these visions and experiences would no doubt be connected to the utterly remarkable person the pre-Easter Jesus was.

However, as time passed and churches continued to be formed and developed, christological images of Jesus evolved, many of them with increasingly divine qualities, such as Son of God, Messiah, Wisdom of God (Sophia), Lord, lamb of God. Rooted in Jewish tradition, these images are metaphors. John's gospel added a number of metaphors to this list: light of the world; good shepherd; the way, the truth and the life; bread of life; the vine; and so forth.

It is important to remember that christological images of Jesus are confessional, metaphorical language about him, not statements of fact. They are post-Easter images growing out of the faith communities. They are the voices of the communities, not the voice of Jesus. I do not believe that Jesus ever made these sorts of claims about himself. To begin with, he never claimed to be God. The "I am" statements about Jesus in John's gospel are metaphorical; they are the voices of the community about Jesus (recorded some seventy years after his death), not Jesus' voice about himself.

Still, as the years passed, images of Jesus continued to evolve, nudging him closer to a oneness with God. While I do not believe Jesus was divine, nor do I believe Jesus thought he was divine, language about Jesus' divinity and oneness with God became increasingly normative. And although it was originally metaphorical, as the voice of the community about the post-Easter Jesus (which should never be taken literally), conservative-evangelical Christianity of our day (and for many decades) makes no distinction between the post-Easter voice of the community and the pre-Easter Jesus. Along with this, because conservative-evangelical Christianity continues to be the dominant voice of Christian faith in our nation, Jesus' divinity has become a cornerstone of what people believe when they think of the Christian faith.

For me and countless others within progressive Christian circles, this is a huge problem. It is a problem not only because it presents a Jesus who is not believable but also because the conclusions it makes about Jesus as a human person, growing out of a literal reading of the Bible, are highly suspect and do not represent the best of modern biblical scholarship.

Pre-Easter and Post-Easter Controversies

The pre-Easter Jesus is Jesus of Nazareth, the fully human, real person who lived, suffered, and died. The post-Easter Jesus is who Jesus became in the years after the resurrection as the early Christian communities evolved in their experience and understanding of him.

As we look back, Jesus is both of these persons/realities. Yet how we understand the different controversial issues of our Christian story depends largely on whether we view the issue from the perspective of the pre-Easter or post-Easter Jesus. The pre-Easter Jesus is based on history remembered that evolved into history metaphorized. In other words, the gospel writers took what the oral tradition passed on to them and incorporated it into the metaphorical narrative of their gospel accounts. Again, remember that the gospel authors were looking back into history some forty to seventy years.

The Miracles of Jesus

While Jesus might well have actually done some of the miracles (e.g., paranormal healings), he probably did not actually do most of the miracles attributed to him in the gospels. We should note that in the Christian tradition, there are no miracles mentioned in any of the biblical narratives until the eighth decade CE. In other words, in the writings of Paul (which predate the gospels by ten to twenty years), as well as with the pseudo-Pauline letters (attributed to Paul but clearly not written by him), there is not a word of Jesus as a miracle worker. I guarantee you that the overwhelming majority of modern Christians are totally unaware of this.

Clearly Jesus' activity as a miracle worker is a creation of the gospel writers themselves. We need to remember that the early Christian communities out of which the gospels emerged were exclusively Jewish. Thus—again, forty to seventy years after the crucifixion—when the gospel writers wanted to cast Jesus as the *new* Moses, their Jewish audiences would understand.

Just as Moses had special power over water in the crossing of the Red Sea, the gospel writers have Jesus walk on water. Where Moses orchestrates feeding the Israelites in the wilderness experience with manna from heaven, Jesus feeds the five thousand with but two fish and five loaves. These events were *not* understood in a literal way by their Jewish-Christian listeners. It was only later, in the mid-second century and beyond, when the Christian church had become virtually all Gentile, that people began to understand these miracles in a literal way.

Other miracles associated with Jesus emerged out of the Jewish messianic tradition. The Messiah would be the one who would usher in the age to come, an age marked by wholeness, not brokenness; by healing, not sickness; and by the power of life reigning supreme over the power of death. Isaiah 35 had spoken of this in dramatic language. It would be a day when the blind would see, the deaf would hear, the lame would walk, and the mute would sing. Over time, as Jesus came to be viewed as the Messiah, the gospel authors wrapped these age-to-come signs around the ways they spoke about him. This was all metaphorical narrative of course, never intended to be taken literally.

In addition to this, as the years passed, increasingly, divine qualities were attached to Jesus. Memories and experiences of him, along with feelings about him, influenced the ways people thought of him, to the point where miracles linked to him took on a natural air. The language of miracle became a metaphor for how people felt about him and for the life-changing role the post-Easter Jesus played in their lives.

The Second Coming

I cannot imagine the pre-Easter Jesus, the historical Jesus, ever thinking about a Second Coming. He was way too consumed and occupied in faithfully living out his *first* coming. Only in the context of the developing Christian communities would the idea of a Second Coming ever gain any traction. The Second Coming is almost certainly a totally post-Easter phenomenon.

As I noted earlier, for many the Second Coming was a natural outgrowth of the apocalyptic eschatology (related to the end of the world) that sprung up after the devastating war with Rome in 70 CE, where Jerusalem and the Temple were utterly destroyed. Again, Judaism had long held that the resurrection of the Messiah would spawn some end-of-time event.

Beyond this, in post-Easter communities, where passionate belief in Jesus as personal Savior was so strong, situations where feelings about him were so heightened and real, it was not much of a leap for people to begin to link their ideas of salvation to Jesus' hoped-for return. Certainly it would be a very popular way to understand salvation.

A more likely scenario would be that the prospect of the Second Coming was rooted in a social hope, hope for a better day, a day of greater justice and fairness for the peasant class, for those marginalized by the oppressive ways of the domination system. In this sense, the Second Coming was a post-Easter metaphor for a more just world.

Lastly, an alternative view put forth by former Episcopalian bishop and author John Shelby Spong suggests the Second Coming happened when the already resurrected Jesus breathed on the disciples in the third resurrection narrative of John's gospel (John 20:21–22).[4] Of course, the Gospel of John is itself post-Easter metaphorical narrative and should never be read in a literal manner.

Jesus Died for Our Sins

I do not believe the pre-Easter Jesus died for our sins, at least certainly not from his point of view. Nor do I believe that Jesus' death was part of God's plan or in any way an expression of God's will. What kind of a God would will the brutal death of such a good and loving person?

However, from the vantage point of the post-Easter Jesus, I do believe that God could use Jesus' death—however horrific and unjust—for good. I believe God does what God can to use all evil for good. In other words, I believe that God (where God is understood as energy, spirit, love, and mystery) used Jesus'

---

[4]John Shelby Spong, *The Fourth Gospel: Tales of a Jewish Mystic*, pages 295–296, 2013, HarperOne.

death to invite a *new turning* in people (a repentance), a turning away from the old way; a return from exile. From the point of view of the post-Easter church, Jesus' death and resurrection can prompt in people a dying to an old way of being and a rebirth to a new way of being. In this sense, the Christian life is an ongoing personal transformation.[5]

Jesus is God

As I have noted multiple times, I do not believe that Jesus is God, nor do I believe that Jesus thought he was God. Jesus may have wondered at times about the meaning of the God presence in his life (i.e., the way God was in him), about what it all meant and where it might lead. That would be understandable. However, I do not believe that Jesus of Nazareth, the historical Jesus, would ever have confused himself with God.

Commenting further on this, if you think about this logically, Jesus would have to have been a crazed, delusional person to think he was God. For a man of his character and humble spirit, this sort of claim would have been way over the top; there is nothing in the pre-Easter tradition to support such a claim.

However, as mentioned before, for the post-Easter communities of faith, as time elapsed understandings of Jesus and interpretations of who he was continued to evolve. As the decades passed, belief about Jesus increasingly took on divine qualities. New layers of interpretation in the gospels were, of course, metaphorical, culminating with the Gospel of John, which I believe to be virtually all metaphorical narrative.

Keep in mind that just because something is metaphorical does not mean it is not true, or less than true. Oftentimes it is even *more* true, which is what I would say about metaphorical narratives in the gospels, particularly in John's gospel. For me, John's gospel, metaphorical as it is, is the most revealing of all the gospels. Because of its metaphorical nature, among the gospels, it gives us

---

[5]For a fuller discussion of this, see chapter 2, pages 41–42.

the most concrete insight into who Jesus was for the evolving church as well as offers creative language for the sustaining power of the Christian faith.

For example, consider the insightful prologue in John, where the poetry invites us in:

> *What has come into being in him was life, and the life was the light of all people. The light shines in the darkness, and the darkness did not overcome it.* (John 1:3–5)

And the richly metaphorical and prompting "I am" statements about Jesus: "I am the bread of life" (John 6:35); "I am the light of the world" (John 8:12); "I am the good shepherd" (John 10:11); "I am the resurrection and the life" (John 11:25); "I am the way, and the truth, and the life." (John 14:6)

The metaphors of John touch intuitive feelings in us that warm our hearts and take us deeper into God. Jesus is indeed the way and the truth; he is the light that no darkness can put out. Nicodemus comes out of the darkness seeking this light. The Samaritan woman at the well seeks this same light. Lazarus comes out of the grave of death to embrace this light. The light draws us in and reassures us that it's all about love, "that we may all be one" (John 17:21).

Jesus is Lord

The pre-Easter Jesus, the historical Jesus, the Jesus who walked the earth like you and I walk the earth, did not think of himself as Lord and had no sense that he would ever be viewed as Lord. This is a totally post-Easter appellation.

As the early centuries unfolded, increasingly Jesus came to be viewed as the Messiah. Given the well-known messianic tradition within Judaism, this is not surprising. At the same time, the idea of Jesus as Messiah held little meaning for the Gentiles. As the Christian church evolved and became increasingly Gentile, *Jesus is Messiah* gradually gave way to *Jesus is Lord*. As it turned out, this caused huge problems. The term *Lord* has all sorts of divine and supernatural connotations associated with it. And it wasn't long before creedal statements about the Incarnation and the Holy Trinity emerged, making it all the more difficult to view Jesus as human.

This was a post-Easter development growing out of evolving beliefs about Jesus in the communities of faith in the late first century, second century, and beyond.

Are You Saved?

Salvation talk is always potentially problematic in the church. Generally, when conservative-evangelical Christians talk about salvation, they are talking about who is *in* versus who is *out*. "Are you saved?" they like to ask. This emphasis on in-group/out-group tilts understandings of salvation away from its deeper meaning. At a deeper level, salvation is about wholeness, both for the individual and the community. The emphasis is also on *this* life, in *this* world in the here-and-now.

At its best, our Christian faith is not about a list of requirements—Are we doing the right things to be saved? It is a faith that invites us on a lifetime journey into wholeness and eventually beyond death into God. As we think about the afterlife, there is no actual place called heaven. As an idealized spiritual state, heaven has meaning. But its meaning is in the wholeness it calls us to as individuals and communities.

For his part, Jesus shows little interest in heaven or the afterlife. He is interested in the everyday lives of people. With regard to the Bible, salvation is a this-world reality. It is about an unfolding process of becoming more aware and more alive, more healed and more whole.

The Developing Tradition

In summary, it is important that we understand the pre-Easter and post-Easter Jesus as a blended, total picture of who Jesus was and is. This blending is itself part of the developing tradition about Jesus for people of faith, both in and outside the church. This developing tradition is an ongoing process of religious experience, interpretation, and understanding.

THE HUMANITY OF JESUS

One of my primary reasons for writing this book is to place greater emphasis on the humanity of Jesus. Looking at the church and its future, there is a lot at stake in this. Again, at the core of my concern is the huge divide biblical literalism has caused in the church, particularly over the last fifty years.

As an enthusiast for the progressive church, I suggest we read the Bible (1) in light of its historical context and (2) as metaphorical narrative (symbolic language). When this is *not* the case, when we read the Bible literally, when we confuse the pre-Easter Jesus with the post-Easter Jesus, we end up with a Jesus that many twenty-first-century people cannot relate to or believe in.

When the church presents Jesus in theological and christological language that is *not* believable (a consequence of taking the Bible literally), understandably there are going to be consequences for the church. As the months and years pass by, people in the pews start to question what they hear on Sunday mornings and begin to drift from the church. More still, first-time visitors and prospective believers are turned off. Sometimes they don't even know why. "Something just didn't sound right," they'll say. "It didn't feel right." As a commentary on this, I can generally tell within five minutes of a worship service if the language of the church (i.e., the way Jesus and the faith are presented) is going to be a problem for me.

Greater emphasis on the humanity of Jesus helps bring Jesus, the real human person, more alive to us. It makes us appreciate more the depths of his human qualities, the reaches of his compassion and love. He becomes more concrete and real for us.

Part of the problem in believing Jesus is divine is that, over time, his human qualities become diminished. If he is divine, his traits as a human person become more abstract. They seem less real and carry less weight. He becomes less *one of us*. If he is divine, how real can his suffering be, and therein his humanity? All of which makes it more difficult for us to identify with him.

If Jesus did not really struggle with what it means to be human—namely, that we are all going to die; that no matter what we do, we cannot hold off death—then how can God use him to transform us and make us whole? For God to transform us and make us whole in and through Jesus (through the birth of a new awareness and new consciousness, which is what salvation is all about), we must be able to fully identify with Jesus as a human being, as one who has truly shared the depths and the realities of our human journey.

As a Fully Human Person, Who Was Jesus?

What was it like to be Jesus? I confess that I am fascinated by this question; I would really like to know. What was it like to be Jesus of Nazareth? My guess is that the truth is very complex. How could it not be? And of course, we can never know.

The starting point for me is my curiosity and wonder about the God presence that was in Jesus—the gripping sense he must have experienced of God, or the Spirit, being present in him. What must it have been like? How old was he when he first noticed this God presence in him? (I refer to this as a *God presence* for want of a better descriptive term. It is the very real sense that God, or the Spirit, is a vital presence in oneself.) Again, what must it have been like?

How did it affect the way Jesus interacted with his family, his peers, and his community? How did it affect the ways he thought about himself? Did he think he was weird (which he probably was in some ways)? Did he feel misunderstood, as if he didn't fit in (which he probably didn't in some ways)?

I can imagine some awareness of this God presence in Jesus at an early age, as a young boy. Yet again, what was it like and how did it evolve? We can never know; nonetheless, for him it must have been very real. At some point, this God presence must have planted the idea in his mind and spirit of some sort of God-inspired, religious activity and life purpose.

Assuming that Jesus really did talk about the kingdom of God and how it had come near; and that he had a relationship with John the Baptist and, to whatever extent, admired John and viewed him as a mentor, how did all of this come about? How was all of this nurtured in his mind, heart, and spirit? Based on Mark's gospel, along with Matthew and Luke, I'm not sure the pre-Easter Jesus ever actually knew John that well. I do think Jesus admired him and was, in some way, drawn to him.

And what about his relationship with his family, with his parents and siblings? Was Jesus a difficult child? Was he hard to raise? Did his parents lose sleep worrying about him, wondering what was going on in his spirit? Fascinating questions!

And what about his siblings? Given what we know, he must have been close to James. But what was it like for James along the way, as Jesus evolved and grew, and as Jesus' mission and revolutionary spirit began to take shape? Who knows what conversations the brothers shared! And who knows how difficult it must have been for James (and Jesus' other siblings as well) to witness Jesus as his ministry unfolded and as the challenges mounted before him.

It is hard for me to conceive of Jesus *not* being an odd person at some point (if not at many points) along his maturation process. Trying to sort out the meaning of the God presence and what it all meant might well have tormented him. Who could he turn to for conversation and reflection on any of this, to help him process it and gain some perspective on what was happening?

My guess is that, in the process of discovering who he was and trying to connect it all to the God presence that pulsated in his spirit, Jesus' self-awareness was always growing, always evolving. Certainly his wilderness experience in the gospel stories suggests a wrestling with the shadow side of the human spirit, a sorting out of who he was and how the Spirit was moving in his life as his period of public ministry was bracing to be launched.

In his active ministry, and in his relationship with his disciples, how frustrating was it for Jesus to be who he was, with this God presence constantly alive in him? On numerous occasions in the gospels, particularly the synoptics, Jesus expressed frustration, most notably with his disciples.

In Jesus' hometown of Nazareth, because the people had no doubt known him growing up (and had also known his family), there was apparently a clear resistance to his message. When Jesus tried to talk to his disciples about his probable suffering and death (a clear post-Easter reference in Matthew, Mark, and Luke), Peter tries to rebuke Jesus but ends up being severely rebuked himself. Still later, at Capernaum, Jesus notices the disciples arguing among themselves about who among them was the greatest, as if they were totally clueless about who Jesus was and the ominous forces that were mounting up against him.

To actually *be* Jesus (with this powerful God presence alive in his spirit) in all of these contexts could not have been easy and would, in part, explain the frustration Jesus must have experienced as the pre-Easter Jesus. We cannot help but wonder, besides God, who did he talk to? To whom did he pour out his heart? Who did he seek out for feedback and input on all that was happening to him?

Jesus and Mary Magdalene

When we read *The DaVinci Code* and other stories that suggest a possible intimate relationship between Jesus and Mary Magdalene, we cannot help but wonder. In the big picture (or larger scheme) of things, does it matter? As a real human person like you or me, would it be acceptable if, indeed, Jesus had a burning flame in his heart for Mary? For me, it would not be a game changer. Part of me would be happy for Jesus, knowing that he was able to enjoy intimate relations with a woman. Would not such a relationship be preferable to a life of abject loneliness, to a life where he could never share the more intimate and human elements in his spirit with anyone?

It is certainly possible and even likely that Jesus and Mary had a close relationship. Perhaps she was a person whom Jesus felt he could talk to and share all that was stirring in his spirit. Even if there were never intimate relations between them, still, they could well have shared a special closeness.

Was Jesus a Sinner?

If Jesus was fully human and *not* divine, does this mean that Jesus, like any of us humans, was a sinner? I have a twofold response to this question. To begin with, I do not think this is the right (or the most appropriate) question to ask, not just about Jesus but about any of us.

The terms *sin* and *sinner* are too strong. They are too demeaning. Too much of our Christian tradition packs too great a punch with the term *sinner*. Typically the term is too quickly associated with personal guilt, as if to say, as sinners, we are *bad* people. I understand that *sin* can mean "falling short of the glory of God" and, of course, we all fall short. Still, over all, I do not find the term to be helpful.

A more adequate question: Do we, or Jesus, fall short of the excellence of God? The answer: of course we do; we are not God. We could insert the term *perfection* here instead of *excellence*, except that I am not a fan of perfection criteria in anything because perfection, as a reality, does not exist. It is an elusive abstraction, inherited from Greek philosophy that, given a more process and relational notion of the world (the worldview taken in this book), is not helpful. Again, a better term is excellence.

So now that we have the *right* question, or at least a more adequate question, my second response—my answer to the question, Does Jesus fall short of the excellence of God?—is yes, but not by much. Again, Jesus is *not* God and therefore, ultimately he must be less than God. In conclusion, it is more helpful to think of Jesus as realizing the excellence of God while at the same time *not* actually being God. Jesus is less than God but he is still an extraordinary and remarkable human being. More still, over time Jesus came to be viewed as *the* human being whom faith communities grew to believe God claimed as God's Messiah.

Before leaving the topic of sin, I want to respond to possible concerns some may have that I am being naive or too soft on sin. Do I believe sin exists? Yes, sin exists, and humans sin all the time. Sin is when we do or say things that do not reflect the best of God that is in us. Sin is greed, pride, craving for too much power and control. Sin is self-centeredness run amok. Still, in our dealings with one another, I do not think pointing to our sinfulness is the best starting point.

Clearly we all need God's forgiveness. Still, most of the time what we really need is God's grace, God's patience, kindness, compassion, and love. I think the church's first response to the people of God should not be concern and regret over our sinful nature (the fact that we are human); rather, the church's first response should be an affirmation of God's love and compassion and the gift of life God has given to each of us.

Did Jesus Need God's Forgiveness?

My simple answer to this question is *yes*, and my guess is that Jesus would say he did as well. We cannot confirm this from any actual accounts in the gospels but, given Jesus' poignant humbleness of spirit and given, too, his very active prayer and meditation life, I cannot conceive of him *not* thinking he needed God's forgiveness. To know God as Jesus must have known God would certainly suggest this. Needing God's forgiveness is an integral part of what it means to be human. God's forgiveness is part of God's saving grace, something any of us would hunger for.

Coming to Terms with the Metaphorical, Post-Easter Jesus

The Jesus the traditional church has presented to its faith communities over the centuries *is* the post-Easter Jesus spoken of in metaphorical narrative in the gospels. The problem is that the church has interpreted these gospel accounts literally, making no distinction between the pre-Easter and the post-Easter Jesus. Again, biblical language about the post-Easter Jesus is virtually all metaphorical narrative. Written forty to seventy years after the crucifixion and resurrection, the intent of the gospel writers was to explain and understand who Jesus was (had become) for them. What is important here is to *not* take the gospels literally. Again, when read literally, we end up with a Jesus who is difficult to believe in.

The progressive, emerging church, in both its theology and Christology, needs to make a clear distinction between the pre-Easter and post-Easter Jesus. And it needs to make clear as well that the language used to talk about Jesus and his ministry activity is mostly metaphorical narrative. Again, this does not mean that the narrative about Jesus is *not* true; it simply means it is *not* literally true.

We can talk metaphorically about Jesus being one with God and about his miracles and his marvelous teachings. All of this is language to convey how Christian communities came to experience Jesus over the years. However, this does not mean it is to be understood in a literal way.

JESUS EVOLVED INTO EVERYTHING HE BECAME

When we are able to see Jesus as fully human and free him from the burden of being God, a whole new vision of Jesus begins to emerge. Suddenly we have a Jesus who is more dynamic, more alive and, most importantly, more one of us. As a human being, what can we say about this Jesus?

To begin with, given what we know about the world and the nature of reality—namely, that the world is in a constant process of becoming (becoming something new)—we can say that *Jesus evolved into everything that he became.* This is a profound statement and may well upset many traditional Christians. However, if we can wrap our minds around this notion, it is a very liberating way of seeing Jesus. It is liberating, in part, because it renders a Jesus in whom we can believe.

All forms of life are in a process of becoming. Life is forever unfolding, moving from yesterday to today and soon on to tomorrow and beyond. It is the way of things.

To imagine Jesus growing up and evolving through the years into all he became is an exciting prospect. It presents us with a Jesus who is wonderfully real. Knowing that Jesus had feelings, like we have feelings; realizing that he struggled with questions of personal identity, just like we struggle, makes it easier for us to identify with him.

What Was Unique about Jesus?

By now, you may well be asking: "If Jesus was fully human, like we are human, then what was unique about him? What sets him apart? He isn't just some normal human being; he's the Son of God, the Messiah, the risen Christ, and the light of the world!" Exactly! As the post-Easter Jesus, he is all of these things.

However, beneath all of the iconic, metaphorical images we associate with Jesus is still a real human being. What is unique about the pre-Easter Jesus (in addition to the five general characteristics of Jesus noted earlier) regarding what he was like is all of the following and more:

- He was born at a particular historical time, into a particular social, economic, and religious world.

- The Jewish religious world he was born into had an expectation of a Messiah, an anointed one—one who would come in the tradition of Moses and the prophets and help Israel realize God's promises to her.

- Given the Roman domination system that surrounded Jesus, along with the injustices of peasant life that were everywhere, the times were ripe for the appearance of a revolutionary spirit.

- Most importantly (and we can never fully grasp this), God's Spirit, along with God's love, compassion, grace, and passion for justice, were *in* Jesus in a powerful and compelling way. All of this converged to enable Jesus to be the remarkable and unique person he was.

Finally, a post-Easter affirmation that builds on all of the above:

- As the reality and the meaning of Jesus evolved in the post-Easter Christian communities, over time, christological images and language about Jesus evolved as well. There came a point where, increasingly, these faith communities began to see Jesus as God's Messiah. To their mind-set, God had declared about Jesus: "This is the human being in whom I am most fully revealed." For all of this to unfold as it did required an amazing convergence of events and happenings.

Jesus' Evolution

Jesus wasn't born a Jewish mystic or spirit person; he wasn't born a healer, wisdom teacher, social prophet, or movement initiator. He became all of these things. Having said this, this does not mean that Jesus was not born with a unique disposition for all of these things. He probably was.

Because of all the post-Easter appellations and beliefs attached to Jesus, it may be hard for us, understandably, to get our minds around the idea that Jesus evolved into all that he became. However, if we think about it, accepting that he was not God but a human being makes sense.

Over the months and years, through the unfolding of his life journey, given all the nuances and complexities of his life, he became all these things. He became a mystic. He became a healer and a wisdom teacher. He became a prophet for social justice and the initiator of a movement. These different roles of who he became all took time and effort.

Who knows how Jesus first discovered he could heal people? It may have just happened, as if accidental. Also, the healings may have been psychological more than physical. Given his deep love and compassion for people, along with his closeness to God, his ability to focus on a person and on an affliction must have been remarkable. Most likely this took time and didn't happen all at once. Perhaps he was unsuccessful on occasions along the way. We can only say that, over time, his community came to experience him as a person able to bring healing to people.

It is easier for us to understand Jesus becoming a mystic and a wisdom teacher. No doubt, early on he had a disposition for intuitive insight and, over the months and years, a disposition for seeing God and the sacred in new and compelling ways. We can imagine all of this evolving in Jesus' spirit, a special gift for seeing God and God's purposes in the context of the sacred. As the God presence that was in him continued to grow, we can imagine his intellect, insight (qualities of perception), sensitivity, and wisdom growing as well.

Jesus' evolution as a social prophet is also not difficult for us to imagine. Given his unique relationship to God (again, the God presence that vibrated in his spirit), along with his awareness of the teachings of the prophets in the Hebrew scriptures, Jesus would have had firsthand experience (indeed, he lived in the midst of this every day) of the economic exploitation and political oppression of the Roman domination system in collusion with the Jewish elites. And no doubt it troubled him deeply. He would have been very much drawn into God's relentless passion for social and economic justice and fairness.

But again, this awareness of injustice and its consequences would have evolved in him. Living under the control of the domination system, conviction would have built up in him over the years. We can easily conceive of Jesus, in a gradual yet unbending process, becoming a prophetic voice for God's justice. Given his closeness to God, indeed, how could he do otherwise?

The movement initiator role of Jesus is less clear to me. My guess is that it just happened as a natural consequence of who he had become in these other roles. A couple of things stand out. To begin with, he had his twelve disciples, his built-in helpers and support system. As a mystic and spirit person, and as a healer, wisdom teacher, and social prophet, there was a lot happening around Jesus. Add to this the disciples and we can begin to see how a movement might well evolve around him and in support of him.

Reflection on Jesus evolving can also apply to the post-Easter Jesus of the early and later Christian communities. In this case, obviously it was not the person of Jesus who evolved but the christological images and language about Jesus. The evolution was within these communities themselves where, over time, they began to think of Jesus as Messiah, Son of God, risen Lord, living Christ, Savior, light of the world, and so forth. These appellations were mostly metaphorical images of Jesus, yet they bear qualitative—sometimes very intense—meaning for the individual believer.

Jesus Evolving in the Gospel Stories

Interestingly enough, even though the gospels are mostly metaphorical narrative about the post-Easter Jesus (history remembered and witnessing remembered), there are a couple of stories that suggest Jesus evolved in his own self-understanding.

In Matthew 15 there is the story of Jesus and a Canaanite woman. As it happens, Jesus has gone to the district of Tyre and Sidon, hoping for some personal time away from the crowds. However, unable to escape notice, a woman whose little girl has an unclean spirit hears about him and comes and bows down at his feet. The woman is a Gentile of Canaanite origin. Historically, the Canaanites were looked down on by the Jews. Not only were they Gentiles and therein unclean but they also were the lowest of the Gentiles. She begs Jesus to cast the demon out of her daughter.

Responding to her, Jesus says, "I was sent only to the lost sheep of the house of Israel." The beleaguered woman continues her plea: "Lord, help me." To which Jesus replies, "It is not fair to take the children's food and throw it to the dogs." The woman's answer no doubt stuns Jesus: "Yes, Lord, yet even the dogs eat the crumbs that fall from their masters' table." Almost immediately Jesus says to her, "Woman, great is your faith! Let it be done for you as you wish" (Matthew 15:24–28). And her daughter is healed instantly.

Clearly Jesus' self-understanding regarding the reaches of his healing is enlarged through this encounter. Suddenly he realizes that Gentiles (non-Jews) are God's creation as well, and are worthy of God's love and healing power. In this story, he seems to evolve to a more inclusive understanding of who he is and whom he is to serve.

A similar evolution takes place in the healing of a centurion's servant in Matthew 8. At Capernaum, a centurion (a Gentile) approaches Jesus, saying, "Lord, my servant is lying at home paralyzed, in terrible distress." Jesus responds, saying he will come and heal him. The centurion then says, "Lord, I am not worthy to have you come under my roof; but only speak the word, and my servant will be healed. For I also am a man under authority, with soldiers under me; and I say to one, 'Go,' and he goes . . . and to my slave, 'Do this,' and the slave does it" (Matthew 8:6–9).

Again, Jesus is taken aback by the man's faith, saying, "Truly I tell you, in no one in Israel have I found such faith." Later, to the centurion, he says, "Go; let it be done for you according to your faith" (Matthew 8:10, 13). And the servant is healed in that hour.

JESUS' CRUCIFIXION AND RESURRECTION

At the heart of our Christian faith are Jesus' crucifixion and resurrection. Both historically and theologically, they go together, each a critical and related part of the other. From the start, we need to understand that the crucifixion and resurrection narratives in the gospels are post-Easter metaphorical reflections, looking back forty to seventy years. These accounts should never be viewed, even remotely, in a literal way. In the church, although Easter services of worship far outdistance Good Friday in attendance patterns, still, it is important to affirm once again that they go together.

Without the resurrection, Jesus' crucifixion would be reduced to a tragic and cruel ending to a life we would probably never have heard about. Without the crucifixion, the resurrection would have had no context, no imprint of a remarkable life story lived out against an oppressive domination system.

At the outset, it should be noted that the resurrection was mostly about the birth of a new awareness and new consciousness. Also, it is very likely that this resurrection awareness took place over a period of months and perhaps years. It was not, as the tradition would suggest, an event that took place two or three days after Jesus' death. In the big picture of things, as all of this settles in, we should remember that the resurrection was an attempt to interpret the meaning of the crucifixion.

In retrospect, as one of my seminary professors used to say, the crucifixion is perhaps Jesus' greatest gift to us, while the resurrection is God's greatest gift. Together they symbolize a transformation model of the Christian life, an invitation to an ongoing life of dying and rebirth, of moving from an old way of being to a new way.

Dying-and-Rebirth Model: Four Meanings

Before looking more deeply at both the crucifixion and the resurrection, I want to describe four meanings that are prompted by the dying-and-rebirth model. While these meanings overlap and are interconnected, they are all post-Easter interpretations of the early communities of faith.[6]

Rejection/Vindication

From the point of view of the early church, God's resurrection of Jesus from the dead, however we understand it, makes a powerful statement. It shouts out a resounding NO to the political and religious authorities of the day. It says, "You got it wrong!" Metaphorically speaking, God vindicated Jesus on Easter morning. What the world sought to put to death, in fact, lives still. The realm of the domination system receives a thunderous defeat. The ways of the world are never the ways of God.

The Way of Jesus Is the Way of God

God's resurrection of Jesus (again, where resurrection means the birth of a new awareness and new consciousness) is also an affirmation of the Jesus way, the way of dying to the old way and being reborn into a new way. Indeed, this is the Christian life: a constant process of letting go of yesterday and opening ourselves to the new thing God seeks to do in our lives today. It is a life of unending personal transformation.

As Paul says about himself in his own personal transformation: "I have been crucified with Christ; and it is no longer I who live, but Christ who lives in me" (Galatians 2:19–20). In raising Jesus from the dead, God claims Jesus' way as God's way as well.

---

[6]These four meanings are similar to Marcus J. Borg's five meanings of the completed path of death and resurrection, in his book, coauthored with N. T. Wright, *The Meaning of Jesus: Two Visions* (San Francisco: HarperOne, 2007), 137.

The Redeeming Power of the Cross

Traditional Christianity teaches that Jesus died for our sins. Beginning in the sixth decade of the Common Era, this belief has been a central tenet of Christian faith and belief. As I have already noted, I do not believe Jesus died for our sins, at least certainly not from his point of view. It simply does not make sense. Crucifixion was the idea of the Roman domination system, pure and simple. It was never God's idea. However, although I could never conceive of God willing Jesus' death on the cross, I *can* see how God could use Jesus' death for God's redemptive purposes.

In my view, part of the power of the cross is a mystical quality that prompts a response of repentance (a turning toward God) within us. When we encounter the cross, we graphically recall Jesus' heart-wrenching suffering unto death. This encounter reminds us of our own humanity, of the ways we have personally fallen short of the wholeness and renewal to which God calls us. It prompts in us a repentant spirit, a turning away from our old self and a new opening toward God's ways, which we see revealed in Jesus. In this sense, the cross is a powerful symbol/metaphor of the suffering love of Jesus.

The Power of God to Bring Life Out of Death

Perhaps the most compelling meaning of Easter is that God (the Spirit) brings life out of death. In all things, God is about Life with a capital *L*. Life is what is so sacred to God's spirit. It is God's relentless nature to give life. That is what God (the Spirit) does. When Israel suffered long and hard at the hand of the oppressive Pharaoh, God called her to a new life through the Exodus experience. Centuries later, in Babylonian exile, on the edge of a despair that seemed to know no bounds, again, God called Israel to new life in a dramatic return to Judah and Jerusalem in what is known as the restoration.

God is forever calling us to new life and new hope. The domination system thought it had permanently silenced Jesus' voice and crushed his spirit. Then Easter happened and somehow Jesus was still alive to his disciples and ardent followers. Easter makes two fundamental claims to the world: (1) the God presence in Jesus was so alive and so powerful that it lived on in the life experience of Jesus' followers; and (2) by the grace of God, love is more powerful than death.

Crucifixion

Jesus was fully human. He was not God, even though over the years the post-Easter community attached divine-like qualities to him (history metaphorized) as it looked back on history. One of the reasons Jesus' humanity is so important is that when we see him as totally human, as you or I are human, it makes his suffering and death more real.

More still, Jesus' death was not part of some plan God had to save the world. God did not *will* that Jesus die a gruesome and horrific death on a cross. Jesus was executed by the evils of the Jewish elites and the domination system of Roman imperialism. What this means is that Jesus' death was real. It was *really* real. There is no softening Jesus' suffering and death because it was somehow all a part of God's plan; this would suggest that if God had wanted to, God could have changed plans and rescued Jesus from such a ghastly death.

It should be noted that the idea that Jesus' death on the cross was part of God's plan for salvation is a totally post-Easter interpretation. It was formed over the years and centuries as faith communities, looking back on history, tried to make sense of things. Indeed, the strong emphasis on salvation is itself a later post-Easter development. No where in the gospels, nor in the letters of Paul, is it a major emphasis.

As Christians, it is important that we get our minds and spirits around the harsh reality that Jesus *really* suffered—most likely, suffered excruciatingly—and *really* died a horrific death. Can we possibly imagine what this must have been like? Although virtually all of the words attributed to Jesus on the cross are part of the metaphorical narrative of the gospel accounts of his death, still, I can imagine Jesus, on the cross, really saying something such as: "My God, my God, why have you forsaken me?" His sense of loneliness, despair, and abandonment must have been unspeakably wrenching.

Did Jesus Have to Die on a Cross?

For me, the simple answer is no. Did Jesus have to die at this point in his life, even if it was by some other means? Again, the simple answer is no, but it's complicated. My guess is that if Jesus had wanted to put aside enough of what he believed and quiet his voice against the domination system, he could have stayed clear of Jerusalem and lived a more controversy-free life. But, of course, then he wouldn't have been who he was. He would have been someone else and, most likely, we would never have heard of him.

Even still, I do not think Jesus *had to* die. However, as a social prophet, once he began to continually speak out against the domination system and criticize the Jewish elites, his days were numbered. We need to remember that the Roman world in which Jesus lived was a dangerous world. The emperor and his minions wielded tremendous power. At the end of the day, Jesus' critical words and menacing presence made people in high places (the leaders of Jewish Torah and Roman law) uneasy and angry, eventually prompting them to act against him. Also, in this context, once he decided to go to Jerusalem, for all intents and purposes, his fate was sealed. Jerusalem was known as the city where prophets were killed.

Why Was Jesus Executed?

Simply put, Jesus died because his social justice protests against the Roman domination system upset too many people in positions of authority and power. It was the convergence of the two leading legal systems of the day that put him to death: namely, Roman law and Jewish Torah. Rome crucified him, but Jewish elites were complicit in the process. Both wanted him killed.

It should be noted that these Jewish elites were not the most noble and respected leaders within Judaism. Many of them were too accommodated to the politics and power arrangements of the times. Thus, we Christians should not be too quick to pass judgment on our Jewish brothers and sisters for the death of Jesus. Jesus was a Jew, as were all of his disciples and most of his followers. A modern parallel would be for the rest of the world to judge all Americans based on the politics and actions of a particular American president.

Why Was Jesus Crucified?

Roman rule had a tradition of crucifying people viewed as troublemakers or nuisances to the state. Crucifixion was a public event and was relatively common under first-century Roman law. It was such a gruesome way to die that the Romans used it as a deterrent against those who might consider critical or threatening actions and behaviors against the state.

Did Jesus Think He Had to Die in Order to Achieve His Life Purpose?

According to the gospel writers, Jesus saw his death as an integral part of his life purpose. Indeed, the prophets had spoken of it. Each of the gospel authors has Jesus tell his disciples multiple times about his death and resurrection. In Mark, the earliest gospel, Mark has Jesus say, "The Son of Man must undergo great suffering, and be rejected by the elders, the chief priests, and the scribes, and be killed, and after three days rise again" (Mark 8:31).

Luke's Emmaus Road Easter story adds to this. On the road to Emmaus, after the resurrection, Luke has Jesus appear in spirit to two of his followers. Walking with them a ways and listening to their conversation, Luke has him say, "'Oh, how foolish you are, and how slow of heart to believe all that the prophets have declared! . . .' Was it not necessary that the Messiah should suffer these things and then enter into his glory? Then, beginning with Moses and all the prophets, he interpreted to them the things about himself in all the scriptures" (Luke 24:25–27).

Paul, who predates Mark by about twenty years, has a similar understanding of Jesus' death. In 1 Corinthians 15:3, Paul recalls the tradition he received in his call to be an apostle: "For I handed on to you as of first importance what I in turn had received: that Christ died for our sins in accordance with the scriptures."

In light of these biblical accounts, it is hardly surprising that the early church saw Jesus' death as directly related to the purpose of his life. But did Jesus himself see it this way? Did the pre-Easter Jesus think he had to die so God's purposes could be realized through him? Or are these scriptural accounts post-Easter interpretations of the early Christian communities?

Along with a majority of mainline scholars, I see the passion predictions in Mark and the other gospels as post-Easter interpretations. I do not think Jesus thought he had to die to achieve his life purpose. Such a notion is way too far-fetched. Most likely, Jesus' life purpose was consumed by the God presence that was in him, a God presence that filled him with compassion and love, along with a zeal for social and economic justice.

I cannot imagine Jesus having the time or inclination to worry about some abstract notion of salvation or dying for the sins of the world. These are all post-Easter metaphorical narratives that people felt deeply about as they looked back some forty to seventy years into history in an effort to bring meaning and purpose to their respective faith communities.

I do not believe that any of the atonement theological interpretations of Jesus' death actually go back to the pre-Easter Jesus. I believe they are all post-Easter metaphorical narratives. I understand the logic (that God needs a sacrificial Savior to atone for the sins of humankind). But I think it is mostly bad theology. God's Messiah does not need to atone for the sins of the world. God's Messiah needs to live a life that calls us to be living embodiments of suffering love and compassion that lead to social and economic justice. When we do this, human sin is transcended and God's redemptive purposes and call to wholeness are realized.

Resurrection

As we consider the resurrection, there is always an aura of transcendent mystery that looms over it. As noted above, in recent years there has been an increasing number of progressive scholars who think the resurrection—however we understand it—did not take place two or three days after the crucifixion, as the gospel accounts and the Christian tradition suggest. These voices offer that, very likely, the resurrection took place over a more extended time, perhaps a period of several months, even years.

If we think about it, this would make total sense. After all, what the resurrection is mostly about is the birth of a new awareness and a new consciousness that spring forth as the disciples and Jesus' most ardent followers continue to sort out the reality that Jesus is somehow still alive to them in a powerful way. In other words, they continue to sense and feel his presence as a living reality.

The new consciousness that Easter ignites is a fuller awareness of what it means to be human. What the Easter experience reminds us is that the suffering love that Jesus lived and died into on the cross is God's way. It is what makes us more deeply human. It is the way that offers the highest hope for God's purposes to be realized: that we may all be one.

In the church and in our faith journey, all the time we talk about love, as well we should. But too often our words about love are vague and do too little for us. *Suffering love* packs more power; it is a more directed love. *Suffering love* means we have to make sacrifices, we have to give up stuff, we have to give ourselves to the larger needs of the whole—the whole family, the whole team, the whole church, the whole community, the whole planet.

Interestingly enough, the disciples and Jesus' earliest followers seemed to sense this intuitively. Although we don't know details but only what we can surmise from the gospel accounts, these followers had a new awareness and energy in their spirits. The depth and reaches of Jesus' love—the way God's Spirit was in him—had won their hearts and there was no turning back. Over time, as they shared their experiences and memories of Jesus both in and beyond the synagogue, the Christian church was born. Again, this was a process that took place over time. And the heartbeat of the process, speaking metaphorically, was the suffering love of Jesus that rose from the ashes of Good Friday on Easter morning. This was the larger meaning that gave rise to the resurrection.

About resurrection, of course, people want *to know*; we want to know what happened and that we can believe the claims of the Easter experience—that Jesus lives. In a sense, it is too bad we place so much emphasis on *knowing*. More than knowing, what Easter is about is meanings. Again, mystery is everywhere and at some point we simply have to accept that there is so much we cannot know. Ultimately it is the feeling in the heart that matters, the transformation in the spirit. God's resurrection of Jesus (again, understood metaphorically) is not an event or an experience that lends itself to empirical proof.

The resurrection is not about factual accounts. The Easter stories of the gospels, therefore, should never be read in a literal way. They should be read and experienced as metaphor; looking back into history and into the experience of the faith communities, they are metaphorical narrative. This does not mean the stories are not true. As metaphorical narrative, they are more than true. There is a truth to metaphor that always transcends the truth of what we consider to be actual facts.

What is important in the resurrection stories of the gospels is *not* that we believe they literally happened, as historical events. What is important are their meanings (e.g., the birth of a new awareness and new consciousness). These meanings unfold as we continue to open ourselves to the mystery and transformational power of the Easter experience.

What Was the Context/Real-Life Situation for Resurrection?

Along with the crucifixion, the resurrection of Jesus from the dead is a core affirmation of our Christian faith. Biblical understandings of the resurrection are post-Easter metaphorical narratives. Their intent is to interpret the crucifixion. In order to grasp the magnitude of the resurrection, we have to first seek to understand the historical context. At the heart of the context is Jesus and God's relationship to each other. The resurrection has everything to do with the God presence that was in Jesus; indeed, it builds on the remarkable human person the pre-Easter Jesus was. What do I mean by this?

It was not just any human being who the early believers thought was resurrected by God. It was Jesus of Nazareth in whom God's Spirit, love, compassion, and justice vibrated so strongly. Ultimately, part of the meaning of Easter is that the God presence that was in Jesus was more powerful than death; as spiritual mystery, power, and love, it could not be killed. Certainly part of the uniqueness of Jesus is that God's love, truth, and purposes were alive in him in such life-giving ways.

The resurrection of Jesus has this relational aspect to it. Understood metaphorically, the impetus comes from God; it is God's action. But God needed a human being who could rise to realize God's purposes. In this sense, Jesus had to be sufficiently open to God's Spirit and able to live out God's ways. No easy task. Again, the resurrection is a relational event. For the resurrection to happen, God and Jesus needed a unique personal history that bound them together in spirit. The point is, a lot of things had to come together for the resurrection to take place, starting with the unique human person Jesus was. This is all part of the context for Easter.

The Early Meaning of Easter

The simple meaning of Easter is that Jesus lives. Jesus, who was crucified, who suffered and died on a cross, was still, somehow, a living reality to his followers. We do not learn many details of this until the eighth decade of the Common Era, with Mark. Writing perhaps twenty years earlier, Paul referred to the resurrection but makes no mention of the details or the names of people who experienced it. By the time the gospel writers began to create their gospel accounts, who knows how the stories and memories of the Easter experience had evolved as they were passed on?

Testimonies to the good news of Easter were no doubt gradual, evolving over time. Always, there is so much that we do not and cannot know. For example, how long did it take for the experiential reality and amazement of the good news to become known? What was the time frame? And who knows what the amazement was really about? Remember, these accounts were written some forty to seventy years after the fact.

We cannot help but wonder precisely how Jesus, after his crucifixion, was still alive to his disciples and followers. Or, altering the perspective somewhat, to what extent was the *amazement* really more like a feeling response of the post-Easter communities (i.e., the way they felt Jesus in their hearts) as they continued to affirm his presence as a living reality in their faith communities? What about the recorded appearances of Jesus in the gospel resurrection stories? In what ways were these appearances real? If we free up our imagination and intuitive impulses, appearances in the form of apparitions and visions are certainly conceivable and very probably occurred on multiple occasions.

Still, whatever happened, the evolving faith communities built on the experiences of the believers as the new awareness and new consciousness of resurrection continued to rise up in their hearts and spirits. And as the weeks and months passed, everything changed. But what did it all mean? Amazement! To be sure! Stunned surprise! Absolutely! But now what?

What the Gospels Say Happened

Before looking at the gospel narratives of the Easter experience, we need to remember again that the gospels were written some forty to seventy years after the crucifixion. The gospel stories of Easter might possibly contain some history remembered but the stories themselves are all post-Easter metaphorical narrative. They are the stories of Easter that evolved in the lives of particular faith communities during the forty to seventy years since Jesus' crucifixion.

In Mark's account of Easter, early in the morning, Mary Magdalene and some other women go to the tomb with spices to anoint Jesus' body. Arriving at the tomb, they are surprised to note that the huge stone at the tomb's entrance has already been rolled back. Entering the tomb, they are immediately alarmed to see a young man dressed in a white robe sitting off to the right. The man says to them:

> *"Do not be alarmed; you are looking for Jesus of Nazareth, who was crucified. He has been raised; he is not here. Look, there is the place they laid him. But go, tell his disciples and Peter that he is going ahead of you to Galilee; there you will see him, just as he told you."* (Mark 16:6–7)

Their first reaction is stunned amazement, as we might imagine; and they say nothing to anyone, for they are afraid. Later in Mark, the risen Jesus appears to Mary Magdalene. She shares her experience with some of the others but they do not believe her.

In Matthew, Jesus appears to Mary Magdalene and the other Mary and tells them, "Go and tell my brothers to go to Galilee; there they will see me" (Matthew 28:10). Later, at the conclusion of his gospel, Matthew has Jesus appear to them on a mountain in Galilee, telling them to take the message of repentance and forgiveness of sins to the nations. Matthew's gospel concludes with the familiar words of the risen Jesus, known in the tradition as the Great Commission:

> *Go therefore and make disciples of all nations, baptizing them in the name of the Father and of the Son and of the Holy Spirit, and teaching them to obey everything that I have commanded you. And remember, I am with you always, to the end of the age.* (Matthew 28:19–20)

More than a mandate to convert the heathen, Jesus' commissioning of his disciples is a commissioning to go to the ends of earth, to wherever there are barriers that need to be broken down, to wherever we find the rejected, the marginalized, the vulnerable (in our day, the immigrant, the person of another religious or ethnic tradition, or the person in the LGBTQ community), those who would otherwise be excluded from God's love; go there and extend to them a welcoming hand, inviting them in. This welcoming spirit is all part of the new awareness and new consciousness that grew out of the resurrection experience.

In Luke, it is much the same story, with Jesus appearing to his disciples and even asking for and receiving something to eat, which he ate in their presence. What is most unique to Luke is his instructive account of the walk to Emmaus.

John's account of Easter is the longest of the four gospels. While the story line and characters are much the same, John includes the story about doubting Thomas (John 20:24–29), the "Do you love me?" sequence with Jesus and Peter (John 21:15–17), and the special reference to "the beloved disciple" at the conclusion (John 21:20–25).

The Emmaus Road Experience

Without doubt, Luke's excellent story of the walk to Emmaus is the best Easter story we know. Clearly a metaphorical narrative, it is a well-crafted, remarkable story on multiple levels.

On Easter, most likely in the afternoon, two of Jesus' followers are on their way to a village called Emmaus, some seven miles from Jerusalem. They had yet to experience the Easter moment. As they walk along, suddenly Jesus himself joins them (in spirit), but they do not recognize him. Engaging them in conversation, Jesus soon learns how disconsolate they are at the tragic events of recent days.

Although some of their group had been to the tomb and found it empty, still, they had yet to see Jesus and are utterly grief-stricken as they walk along. Finally, Jesus begins to speak to them about the prophets and the meaning of the scriptures and how the Messiah had to suffer in this way.

More engaged now as they approached the village, they urge Jesus to stay with them, for it is almost evening and the day is turning late. Going into their home, they bring bread to him at the table. Taking the bread, Jesus blesses it, breaks it, and gives it to them. Then, in an Easter moment, their eyes are opened, they recognize him, and he then vanishes from their sight. They are stunned and overjoyed at the same time. Instantly their lives are changed. Easter has come. Quickly, thinking back, they say to each other, "Were not our hearts burning within us while he was talking to us on the road, while he was opening the scriptures to us?" (Luke 24:32). Soon, unable to contain themselves, they are off to Jerusalem to meet with the disciples and tell them of their experience.

For these two followers of Jesus, the Easter moment came in the breaking of the bread. Suddenly their eyes were opened. Then, just as quickly, they recognized him and he vanished. Just as in the Emmaus Road experience, part of the meaning of Easter is that our eyes are opened. Through the experience of Easter, we see as we have not seen before.

So what were these two followers of Jesus experiencing when Jesus first appeared to them on the road but they did not recognize him? Clearly, had Jesus appeared to them in bodily form they would have recognized him. Did Jesus appear to them as a spiritual body? And if he did, what does this mean? When we think about the Emmaus Road experience, the God presence in Jesus seemed to have a transcendent energy that lived on in the spirit of his followers, to the point where they somehow recognized him and knew he was in some way alive to them.

All of this is part of the mystery of the Easter experience. It is what the resurrection narrative unlocks within us. In this sense, the nuances and reality of the post-Easter Jesus are derived from the truth and power (the life-giving energy) of the God presence that lived in the pre-Easter Jesus. Again, the fact that Jesus was such a remarkable and extraordinary human being gives substance and meaning to post-Easter experiences and reflections on him.

How the Early Church Grew and Evolved in Its Understanding of Easter

In trying to grasp who Jesus became for the early church, it is helpful to understand that each community of faith was evolving on multiple levels. This was an unending, developmental process within each of the faith communities.

Imagine what it must have been like to be in a leadership position in one of these early church communities. As we have seen with the apostle Paul and all the issues the churches he helped start had to deal with, this was no small task. There was no manual on church administration. Beyond all of the practical matters, how were they to understand Jesus? What was his relationship to God? After the resurrection, what did it mean to be one of his followers? What language and terms would they use to talk about him?

In reflecting on this, it is interesting to note the impressive list of names used to refer to Jesus. Christological images didn't just appear out of nowhere. They appeared out of very real contexts in the lives of these early communities of faith. As the months and years marched on, increasingly, over time, these evolving faith communities began to attach divine qualities to Jesus. They came to refer to him as Messiah, Son of God, risen Christ, Lord, Word of God, Wisdom of

God (Sophia), lamb of God, servant of God, light of the world, good shepherd, bread of life, and so forth.

These images are virtually all post-Easter metaphors for who the resurrected Jesus became in these early communities of faith. Most modern scholars do not consider that these images, rooted in Jewish tradition, go back to the pre-Easter Jesus. From what we know of the historical Jesus, it is very unlikely that Jesus thought of himself in these terms.

For example, Jesus would never have referred to himself as the light of the world, or as the Wisdom of God, or the lamb of God. Can we imagine Jesus actually saying to his followers, "I am the light of the world"? People who talk about themselves in such language are considered delusional or megalomaniacs.

Nonetheless, these first communities of faith continued to grow in their experiences of Jesus, as well as in their belief in him and reverence for him. As they grew and evolved, more and more they began to see Jesus as *one* with God and with divine-like qualities. If we think about it, this is an understandable process. Again, as post-Easter metaphor, these were evolving reflections.

How I Think of Easter and Explain the Resurrection

To begin with, Easter is utter mystery. It is the power of God, the love of God, the truth of God, the justice of God, the grace of God, and the mystery of God—all at once. So much of it defies belief (the actual physical details) and yet affirms belief (the emerging spiritual affirmations) at the same time. Certainly we want it to be true. We want to believe Easter happened. We want to believe Jesus is still a living reality in our lives. Reflecting on this, if we want to believe Jesus is a living reality in our lives, then he is; and if he *is*, then the new awareness and new consciousness that resurrection evokes is real for us and is part of our faith experience.

In a historical and factual sense, there is so much we can never know. For example, it cannot be historically proven there was a tomb. Most likely there was not. However, looking back at these physical details, do they matter? Reputable scholars think Jesus was simply left to die which, in the Jewish tradition, would be viewed as shameful. From this vantage point, post-Easter accounts of Jesus' death (that include the story of the empty tomb, which imply that Jesus had a proper burial) would be an attempt to honor the tradition of the Jewish burial and to remove any element of shame.

Most moderns (myself included) do not believe in a physical bodily resurrection. It simply lacks believability. Having said this, one thing we do know is that something happened. This is the undeniable reality of Easter: something happened. Somehow, by the power of God, the love of God, the grace of God, the truth of God, and the mystery of God, Jesus was alive to his most ardent followers. They continued to experience him as a living reality. It may well be that this was due to the remarkable human person Jesus was and that the impact his personal life had on his followers was so powerful that the new awareness of the Easter experience simply could not be held back. From this vantage point, it could be said that Easter started before Jesus' crucifixion.

How do we explain the gospel accounts of Jesus' appearances to Mary Magdalene and the other women, and to Peter and John, and his other disciples and followers? I believe there was something about his followers' experience of the God presence that was in Jesus in his lifetime that could not be killed. However we understand this God presence, it was alive to his followers in a real and vital way. My guess is that this presence was experienced on a level of feelings and intuition. They *intuited* Jesus' presence; they *felt* him being present to them. Jesus' spirit, which they had experienced in his lifetime, was alive to them. If we think about it, all of this *is* resurrection experience.

We need to remember that resurrection is not resuscitation. The latter is a *coming back to life again*; the former is an entry into a new kind of existence. For Jesus' disciples and followers, resurrection experiences of Jesus might well have been very real. Whether they were visions, apparitions, or some sort of spiritual presence (that defies definition), they were real and cannot simply be discarded.

In the metaphorical narrative of the gospel stories, testimonies of Jesus' followers experiencing him as a living reality abound. Again, something happened. To repeat because it bears repeating: there was something about the God presence that was in Jesus in his pre-Easter lifetime that his followers continued to experience in his resurrection. Once more, we are reminded of the remarkable and extraordinary person that the pre-Easter Jesus was.

What Kind of a Resurrection?

Was the resurrection of Jesus a physical or spiritual bodily resurrection? Or was it something more still? Beyond the fact that a physical bodily resurrection is not believable, the Bible places greater emphasis on a spiritual bodily resurrection. I cite three diverse examples, all of which should be read as metaphorical narrative (which means this is how the evolving faith communities came to explain it).

In the apostle Paul's Damascus Road conversion experience, a light from heaven flashes around Paul, knocking him to the ground where he hears a voice saying, "Saul, Saul, why do you persecute me?" (Acts 9:4). Later, the voice says to him, "I am Jesus, whom you are persecuting. But get up and enter the city, and you will be told what you are to do" (Acts 9:5–6).

Paul's companions that day heard the voice but saw no one. Certainly if Jesus had appeared to Paul and his fellow travelers as a physical body, they would have seen him. They saw no one. Paul's experience of Jesus that day must have been as a spiritual form of some sort, most likely as a vision.

In 1 Corinthians 15, Paul talks about how with the resurrection of the dead, what is sewn as perishable is raised as imperishable, and what is sewn as a physical body is raised as a spiritual body. The implication is that it is the spiritual body that is resurrected. And perhaps most compellingly, in Luke's Emmaus Road story, when the risen Jesus joins his two disconsolate followers on the road, they do not recognize him. He walks with them, engages them in lengthy conversation; still, they do not recognize him until the breaking of the bread at the table in their home. If his followers could not recognize him, clearly his appearance among them could not have been physical; therefore, in some form, it must have been spiritual.

Paul's experience on the Damascus Road and Jesus' followers' experience on the Emmaus Road are both accounts of Jesus appearing in some spiritual form. He is not recognizable, yet his presence is experienced. Again, the point is that they experience him as a living reality. He is alive to them in some experiential way.

I do not believe we can ever totally reduce Jesus' resurrection (however we understand it and talk about it) to one final form, such as a spiritual bodily resurrection. Obviously, if we had to choose between physical and spiritual, we would opt for the latter, as the Bible seems to suggest. However, in the big picture of things, the mystery and awe of the resurrection always transcend our human attempts to understand and explain it. All we know for sure is that as the truth of Easter began to settle in, everything had changed. It was a new day, a new world, and a new hope.

The Most Compelling Testimony of Easter

As I understand the resurrection, the most compelling testimony to the truth of Easter is the changed lives of Jesus' disciples and followers. The biblical accounts of these life-changing transformations are themselves metaphorical narratives of the post-Easter community. The unfolding reality is that, after the resurrection, the disciples are not the same persons they were before. They are utterly changed. They could never revert to being the same persons they were before their Easter moment experiences.

Take Peter, for example. Before the resurrection, when fear got the better of him, the gospels report that Peter denied Jesus three times and ended up totally abandoning him. We can only imagine the biting guilt and diminished sense of self-worth that ate away at him after this. After the resurrection, Peter is ready to run through walls for Jesus. Over the weeks, months, and years, he becomes a powerful spokesperson for Jesus and ends up dying a martyr's death in living out his faith convictions. As belief spreads about Jesus' resurrection, we can imagine the disciples' renewed sense of confidence and life purpose.

During Jesus' active ministry, much of the time the disciples must have wondered who he was and how things were going to play out with all that was happening around them. As the experience of resurrection came over them, everything had now radically changed. Jesus was somehow alive to them in ways that were real and that they could not deny.

In the days, weeks, and months ahead, the disciples and other followers would have to figure out what this meant. After their experience of Easter, whatever path they chose to follow would have everything to do with the way they remembered the pre-Easter Jesus speaking, acting, and being among them.

Is the Easter Story Believable?

In a sense, this isn't even the right question. The question we should be asking: What do these Easter stories mean? Still, to read the Easter stories in a literal way is highly problematic. It defies logic and reason on virtually every level. Truth be told, we will never know about the tomb, nor about Jesus' body. If we keep pushing on this, how important are the tomb and the body in the big picture of things?

Conservative-evangelical Christianity has an obvious answer to the question of the empty tomb: Jesus' body was resurrected. Along with what is probably a majority of Christians, conservative-evangelicals believe in the *bodily* resurrection. But what about the *spiritual body* that Paul spoke of in 1 Corinthians 15 and that Luke seemed to suggest on the Emmaus Road? The questions go on and on. Still, for most Christians in the progressive, emerging church, the physical bodily resurrection is a tough sell.

I do not believe in a physical bodily resurrection. Nor am I as persuaded as I would like to be in a spiritual bodily resurrection, although the gospel stories and Paul would seem to suggest this. What resurrection means is the birth of a new awareness, a new kind of consciousness. It is a *new kind of existence*. It is entering into a life process of personal transformation, of dying to our old self and being reborn to a new self, day after day. This I believe.

I believe that in some way, Jesus, in the resurrection experience, was alive to his disciples and followers. I believe in any number of Easter moments where his followers experienced him as a living spiritual reality. And, to repeat, the most convincing argument for resurrection and these Easter moments is the transformed lives of his most ardent followers.

Beyond this I leave any final meaning of resurrection and Easter moments to the mystery of God. I do not need anything more. Easter is not about empirical proofs. It is not about *right* belief. Easter is about meanings. It is about the birth of a new consciousness and a fuller sense of what it means to be human.

The Big Picture Meaning of Easter

The meaning of the crucifixion and resurrection of Jesus is that, as followers of Jesus, we are called to live lives of personal transformation. Our lives are to be an ongoing process of dying and rebirth—dying to an old way of being and rebirth into a new way of being. This new way of being is the way of suffering love. Let's take a look at the meaning of Easter from the different points of view of those involved: God, Jesus, the disciples and followers, the post-Easter communities of faith, and us moderns.

God. Easter is God's victory over the domination systems of the earth. It is the resounding defeat of the pharaohs, caesars, and kings of the world. It says to these worldly powers:

> *Your truth is not my truth. My truth is the truth that shines in and through the life of Jesus of Nazareth. Jesus is my Messiah; he is my Christ, my anointed one. The life of Jesus is THE life that most reflects my life, my ways, my truth, and my spirit. If you want to learn about my love, observe the suffering love of Jesus. If you want to know more of my wisdom, listen to the parables and teachings of Jesus. If you want to be informed by my social justice, listen to the passion of Jesus' words of justice and compassion on behalf of the poor and the marginalized.*

Easter is God's decisive action in Jesus of Nazareth. For God, in the Easter experience, love is more powerful than death. In God's resurrection of Jesus, God takes the suffering love of Jesus on the cross and transforms it into the suffering love that realizes God's redemptive purposes in the world:

Death has been swallowed up in victory. Where, O death, is your victory? Where, O death, is your sting? (1 Corinthians 15:54b–55)

Jesus. At the core of Jesus' heart and soul (as the pre-Easter Jesus) was his undying passion to be faithful to the God presence that was in him. I believe Jesus' earthly life was consumed by the life, love, compassion, and social justice of God. Jesus' energy and focus was on trying to be faithful.

For Jesus, I believe Easter was God's resounding confirmation that Jesus' life and suffering love had not been in vain. For Jesus, there must have been some enormous sense of relief; something like: "Wow, I did it! I was faithful until the end. All praise be unto God! I did not turn away from the 'God presence' that was in me. I stayed true to this presence even though it ultimately led me to the cross."

The Disciples and Followers. As we have already noted, for Jesus' disciples and followers, the eventual meaning of Easter was stunned amazement and joy, although this probably took more time to develop than we have been led to believe. They had to be in some sense of surreal disbelief. However, as the energizing reality began to settle in that Jesus was, indeed, a living presence in their experience, their sense of shared responsibility and mission had to be pounding hard in their minds and spirits. For them, the eventual reality of Easter meant they had work to do. They had to take the good news of Jesus' message to the world, and ultimately not just to the Jews but to the Gentiles as well.

For Paul, this meant a riveting commitment for the rest of his life. For Peter and no doubt most of the other disciples, it meant the growing pains of opening themselves to Gentiles coming into their communities of faith. We remember Peter's experience with Cornelius in the book of Acts where Peter, after receiving multiple signs from God, comes to a new awareness: anyone who fears God and does what is right is acceptable to God (Acts 10:35).

For these disciples and followers, it was a new day. But there was an enormous responsibility and mission before them.

Post-Easter Communities of Faith. To begin with, we need to remember that early on, until they were banished from the synagogue (probably in the ninth decade CE), Jesus' disciples and most ardent followers continued to gather in the synagogues, as was their custom, where most likely they shared memories and stories about Jesus and teachings of Jesus.

Imagine being a part of one of these earlier gatherings (which in some instances eventually grew to become distinct communities) that were seeking to be faithful followers of Jesus. We have to remember that for these first evangelists (some of whom were Jesus' disciples, such as Peter and John), there was no precedent. How were they to know what to do?

My guess is that early on they had to fall back on their memories of the pre-Easter Jesus, the Jesus of Nazareth that many of them knew firsthand and with whom they had walked the roadways of Galilee. They had to remember what his life had been about and where his teachings and values had pointed. For them, as they got their footing, Easter would evolve to where it meant making disciples of people, calling people to a baptism through repentance and forgiveness of sin. They would have seen this as being in the tradition of John the Baptist and Jesus.

At some point along the way, they would have to figure out what they believed about Jesus and what message they wanted to pass on to the new converts in their gatherings and communities. This is where the role of the apostle Paul would become so important and pivotal in the formation of the early church.

Us Moderns. For us modern Christians, and for the contemporary church, I see Easter having two basic meanings. To begin with, it is always the most celebratory and well-attended worship experience of the calendar year. People fill our sanctuaries on Easter morning. The celebrations, with their exalted music and creative liturgies, warm our hearts and lift our spirits. On Easter, good news is all about.

As we find our way home from these Easter services, we are reassured once again that hope is alive, that the truth and suffering love of Jesus' life lives on, and that God has stunned the world with the reaches of God's love.

A second meaning of Easter goes deeper and demands that we view Easter through the suffering love of Jesus at his crucifixion. It asks that we remember the one who suffered and died on the cross. It asks that we remember the size of his love and his compassion for the needy, the sick, the marginalized, and the oppressed. It asks that we remember his passion for God and the kingdom of God, and for social and economic justice for all people.

This meaning of Easter calls us back again to the pre-Easter Jesus and to the life that he lived. It invites us to remember how Jesus was with people—the extended hand and the eager heart of an inclusive love. It invites us to remember his courage to speak truth to power that God's purposes be realized in all things.

In the shadow of the cross, this meaning of Easter reminds us that to be a follower of Jesus is to live a life of dying to an old way of being and being reborn to a new way of being. It means being passionate about God's ways and God's justice in the face of the domination systems of the earth.

In our contemporary world here in the United States, symptoms of our modern-day domination system include the greed of corporations, the disdain for modern science as it applies to global warming and other protections of the environment, and a resistance to reforms in gun ownership, campaign finance, minimum wage, voter suppression, immigration, and education. In our own day, uncontained greed, racial tension, indifference to the poor (to the point, even, of blaming the poor for their own plight), and immediate gratification in everything are troubling characteristics of our times, working against the ways of God.

In response to this, the ways of God and Jesus, which are the ways of suffering love, continue to challenge us and invite us to life. They invite us to be alive to an inclusive love; to kindness, compassion, and generosity. They invite us to be open and welcoming of all people, in particular to the needy and the vulnerable. The best of Jesus reveals the best of God; and together they nudge us all to the spiritual high ground of God's purposes: that we may all be one.

CHAPTER 6

WHERE DO WE GO FROM HERE?

In my lifetime, it seems the church has forever been at an enduring cross-roads. At the center of the crossroads is the problem with biblical literalism in Christianity in general, and in the church in particular. In this book I have tried to make two major points:

1. Biblical literalism poses a very real problem, both for the church and for the integrity of Christianity as one of the major religions of the world. The scope of this problem cannot be overstated. Reading the Bible in a literal manner, as if it were the infallible, inerrant Word of God, threatens the very future of the Christian faith.

Continuing to present the Bible, God, and Jesus in ways suggested by a literal reading of our sacred biblical texts increasingly renders the Christian faith less truthful, less relevant, and less believable for future generations. Over time, as generations come and go, this poses a serious problem and challenge for both Christianity as a religion and for the Christian church.

2. The Bible, when not restricted, distorted, and reduced by the constraints of biblical literalism, is not only eminently believable but also wonderfully rich as a collection of the best stories we know in Western civilization. The Bible is our sacred story; it is our scripture. Unshackled from biblical liter-alism, free to breathe through the vibrant metaphor of its stories, it offers us timeless wisdom, moral and ethical teaching, and profound insight into our ongoing pursuit of the meaning of life.

The Bible you didn't know you could believe in is precisely the Bible I have sought to breathe new life into in this book. As I tried to point out in chapter 1 "The Importance of How We Read the Bible," it is important to read the Bible:

    a. in light of its historical context (i.e., contextually)

    b. as metaphorical narrative (or, as symbolic language)

A derivative problem—in the church and in our wider American culture—is that our language about the Bible, God, and Jesus is the language we inherited from conservative-evangelical Christianity's belief that the Bible is the infallible, inerrant Word of God. And thus we talk about God as the God of supernatural theism, an actual being out there somewhere overseeing life here on planet earth. We talk about Jesus as divine as well as human, and about stories and myths in the Bible as if they were events that actually happened (e.g., the nativity stories of Matthew and Luke, the miracles of Jesus, and the gospel narratives of the Easter experience).

In other words, the language we use in the modern church, for the most part, remains the language of biblical literalism. We talk casually about salvation as if it actually happens as a literal event, about heaven as if it were an actual place, and about Jesus dying for our sins—a morbid way of looking at Jesus. In our conversation about the Bible, we refer to it as the Word of God, knowing full well that the Bible is not a divine product; the Bible was written by human beings.

What this means, of course, is that the language we use to talk about the Bible, God, and Jesus is oftentimes—for increasing numbers of people in our churches and in our wider American culture—language that is flat, short-sighted, and simply not believable. Moreover, this language leads to all sorts of distortions that are harmful and not useful. Easily, the Bible can be reduced to a hammer or a club as a means of control. Biblical texts, taken out of context and not viewed metaphorically, can lead to hurtful conclusions for women, the LGBTQ community, and non-Christians of all stripes. What this suggests is that the language of biblical literalism has consequences that are not helpful to the integrity and the future of our Christian faith.

In many mainline churches, where most clergy do not read the Bible in a literal way, language used about God in prayers and liturgy suggests a God of supernatural theism. For example, countless mainline Christians continue to think of God as intervening in some tangible, supernatural way in response to prayer requests. They think God's will (because God has supernatural powers) determines what actually happens in life, as if it were preplanned by the Almighty.

Language about Jesus is no less problematic. Again, even in our mainline churches (that are more likely to be progressive in their thinking on God and Jesus), many Christians continue to think Jesus is God. They continue to believe that Jesus literally died for our sins and will come again in some form of Second Coming, as a literal reading of the scriptures suggests.

Many of these same Christians also believe in much of what the Christian tradition suggests is true in the nativity stories (i.e., that Jesus was born in Bethlehem and that actual magi from the East followed his star and came to offer special gifts) and the Easter narratives (i.e., that there really was an actual empty tomb and that the somehow risen Jesus physically appeared to the disciples and interacted with them). These post-Easter metaphorical examples emphasize again the importance of making a distinction between the pre-Easter and the post-Easter Jesus.

UNDERSTANDINGS OF THE BIBLE, JESUS, AND GOD ARE ALWAYS EVOLVING

In this concluding chapter, I want to emphasize once again how the Christian faith and the church are always evolving; they are always in a process of becoming something new, something different.

This is a good thing, of course, because always, it seems, we have a ways to go. For example, even with all the progress we have made in race relations in our nation, the Sunday morning worship hour is still the most segregated hour in America. In both the Catholic Church and within most of conservative-evangelical Christianity, women continue to struggle to gain equal footing. Indeed, the church needs to evolve; it needs a fresh glimpse of what it can be—a heartened intrusion of something new, something different. This is no less true for our understanding of the Bible, as new findings and advances in research continue to inform us.

Along with our evolving understandings of the Bible, particularly with regard to the gospels, comes a similar evolution in the way we see Jesus. As post-Easter communities of faith, our experience and understanding of Jesus are always evolving, always unpacking for us deeper insights into who he was, how he was understood in his time, and what he continues to mean for Christians today.

In this vein, greater emphasis should be placed on the implications of Jesus' humanity, particularly as it relates to suffering love. While it is important to acknowledge that the pre-Easter Jesus did not think of himself as divine, at the same time I can understand how post-Easter communities of faith, over time, have ascribed divine qualities to Jesus. However, reflections in these communities on who Jesus was are all metaphorical narrative seeking to capture the experiences and understandings of who Jesus, over time, has become for them.

What is important is that, as Christians, we do not have to believe Jesus was God in order to be Christian. Indeed, when we think about it, when Jesus is freed from the burden of being God, he is better able to reveal for us the very real depths and truths of what it means to be human.

Jesus' humanity is most fully revealed in the way the God presence that filled his spirit influenced the way he interacted in community life; in the way he embraced the poor and the downtrodden; the way he spoke out and took a stand for social and economic justice. Ultimately, this God presence became "lived out" as the suffering love that led Jesus inexorably to the cross.

Although perceptions of God are not as dependent on the Bible as perceptions of Jesus, our ways of understanding God, too, continue to evolve as the years march on. While God is always *more* than our understandings and assessments about God, this is part of what makes the idea and reality of God so engaging for the human spirit. With God, what is important is not what we think we know about God. What is important is the meaning that redounds to us in the process of living our lives into the mystery, wonder, grace, and love of God.

THE CHALLENGE FOR THE CHURCH

Within our progressive congregations, we need to do a better job of making the distinction between a literal reading of the Bible and a metaphorical reading of our sacred texts. Moreover, with regard to the synoptic gospels—and this is a huge issue—we need to emphasize how Christianity began as a movement within the synagogue.[1] As advances in scholarship progress, we are coming to understand how the synoptics were written from a largely Jewish perspective, within a Jewish worldview, based on writings with which only a Jewish person would be knowledgeable. Once more, it is important to make the distinction between the pre-Easter and the post-Easter Jesus.

For the progressive church to truly *be* progressive in the way it presents the Bible, God, and Jesus to its congregants, local church pastors will need to play a major role. In ways that work for them and their congregations, they will need to pay more attention to the language they use personally as well as that used in the liturgical and prayer life of their churches. This awakening to the language the church uses about the Bible, God, and Jesus—in conversation and in worship—will take time and needs to be viewed as a process. Indeed, as a process, it should not be oppressive or insensitive to the natural resistance that will rise up in response to suggested changes. At the same time, pastors and church leadership need to be as proactive as they can in helping their congregations become more knowledgeable and open to exploring for themselves the truth and power of a nonliteral approach to the Bible.

Transitions in language take time, sometimes long periods of time. Important to the process are enlightened Bible study classes where the pastor/teacher can point out the importance of *how* we read the Bible. This book suggests the Bible be read (1) contextually, in light of its historical and social context, and, (2) metaphorically, or as symbolic language. Again, differences should be pointed out between the pre-Easter and post-Easter Jesus.

In dealing with the challenges biblical literalism continues to present for the Christian faith in general and for the local church in particular, the local

---

[1] See John Shelby Spong, *Biblical Literalism: A Gentile Heresy* (San Francisco: HarperOne, 2017).

church has a critical responsibility. Local churches continue to be *the* sacred space where many Christians and seekers (persons interested in learning how they can relate their lives to something larger than themselves) learn about their faith. It is where meaningful teaching and conversation on the life of faith take place. The role of the local church pastor in this unfolding process cannot be overstated. Again, what is at stake is that the Bible, God, and Jesus are presented to people in ways that are authentic and truthful in the multifaceted life of their church experience. The view presented in this book is that when this happens, both the Christian faith and the Bible are eminently believable and, together, continue to be a rich source of inspiration and meaning for countless millions of Christians and prospective Christians around the world.

A VISION FOR CHRISTIAN LIFE

When I think about the Christian faith and the essence of the Christian life, I am reminded how it's all about the love. Love is the key. Love undergirds and flows through everything we seek to be and do as Christians. But it is not just any love; it is the suffering love of Jesus that Jesus lived into at his crucifixion. Always, the cross is at the center of our faith story as Christians.

The way of suffering love is the way where we do what is best for the whole— for the whole family, the whole team, the whole group, the whole church, the whole community, the whole nation, and the whole planet. Always there is a sacrificial element involved, which means we gotta give up stuff; we have to make personal sacrifices. We have to get beyond ourselves into the larger spirit of what it means to be a relational person—a person in relationship to God, to family and friends, to neighbors, and to the wider national and international community.

The Christian life is an ongoing life of personal transformation. In the largest sense, this is what Christian salvation means; it is what it points us toward. It is a life centered in God, a dying to our old self and a rebirth to a new self. Over time, this personal transformation leads to the transformation of community and the world.

Christianity Is Not about "Right Belief"

At its best, the Christian faith is not about *right belief.* The problem with placing too great an emphasis on belief is that, too easily, it reduces Christianity to a list of guilt-inducing requirements, which contradicts the healthy emphasis Christian faith places on God's grace. Grace, given freely and generously, is a core element in our faith. God's grace suggests God's unconditional acceptance of us—flaws and all—as human beings. Its initiative comes from God and the magnificence of God's love, and not from us. Rather than right belief, Christian faith is about the ongoing transformation of our relationships to God, to Jesus, and to one another.

The emphasis on right belief in the church stems from the impulse within conservative-evangelical Christianity to control and manipulate people's behaviors. Leaders within these circles of faith tend to obsess over *right* responses to questions such as: Do you believe the Bible is the Word of God? Are you saved? Do you believe Jesus is the Son of God? That he is born of a virgin? And that he died for your sins and will come again in the Second Coming?

These sorts of *closed* questions give the impression they are initiation rights; they do nothing to stimulate curiosity or self-discovery of who we are as evolving Christians. More still, so-called right responses to these questions say nothing about a person's heart, character, or spirit. A person could easily nod in the affirmative to all of these questions and still be a jerk and an insensitive, uncaring person. Again, Christian faith is about relationship. Most importantly, it is about relationship with God. Living a life centered in God is the life modeled by Jesus himself and is the life toward which he points us.

A life centered in God naturally seeks a life full of God. The possibilities for deepening and transforming relationships here are endless. Such a life is not about perfection or living a sinless life. It is about relationships and a big spirit; and it is about the transformation offered by relationships centered in God. Always, such a relationally based life is about love: the love of God and the suffering love of Jesus that give our lives infinite meaning and purpose.

WHAT IS GOD LIKE?

God is *more* than anything we can ever say, think, or believe about God. Always, God is *more*. Indeed, it is this ever-elusive *more* quality that elevates God in our minds, hearts, and spirits. In the largest sense, God is Spirit. God is also the boundless energy of love in the world. And, to repeat, God is endless mystery.

Christians See God Reflected through Jesus

For Christians, questions about what God is like point unmistakably to Jesus. We believe Jesus gives us a glimpse of God's nature and essence. A glimpse, of course, is only partial. Still, it is a starting point. For Christians, Jesus' ways— his teachings, wisdom, compassion, commitments—reflect God's ways as well.

In reflecting on this, we need to remember that all of these salient traits of Jesus reveal the depths of his humanity. As noted earlier, through his wilderness ex- perience Jesus had an evolved self-awareness. He knew who he was. He had deep personal insight into the depths and the shadows of his human spirit. It was the depths of this very personal, human insight and awareness that gave Jesus the capacity and means to inspire and show us the way to God.

God Is Both Personal and Present

With God, relationships are primary. It is in this sense that God is personal. Indeed, God is the sum and more of all God's relationships. God works in and through relationships. While it is not God's nature to work independently of relationships, God's Spirit of compassion and love work compellingly in and through people. Because God is Spirit, God is everywhere. Indeed, there is no place where God is *not* present. Wherever it is that life exists, God is there working in and through relationships, calling people to life and to love.

God Is Compassionate

The God of our Christian faith is a God of infinite compassion. Indeed, for us Christians, compassion is the essence of God; it is *the* quality about which God is the most passionate. God's compassion is universal, reaching out to every human being on the planet. To know that God *feels* with us in our human endeavors and human plight is both reassuring and inspiring. We see God's compassion reflected in and through Jesus. In the gospel stories, Jesus' first response to any human affliction, pain, or suffering is compassion.

In Mark's story of the feeding of the four thousand, Jesus sees the huge crowds who have been following him and, knowing they have had nothing to eat, he says to his disciples:

> *I have compassion for the crowd, because they have been with me now for three days and have nothing to eat. If I send them away hungry to their homes, they will faint on the way—and some of them have come from a great distance.* (Mark 8:2–3)

Compassion overflows from his heart. Deeply, personally, he cares for people. In Luke 7, when Jesus approaches the town of Nain, he sees a man who has died being carried out from the town. The man's mother, a widow, is weeping uncontrollably. Seeing the woman in pain, Jesus has compassion for her and says:

> *"Do not weep." Then he came forward and touched the bier, and the bearers stood still. And he said, "Young man, I say to you, rise!" The dead man sat up and began to speak, and Jesus gave him to his mother.* (Luke 7:13b–15)

Jesus' compassion reflects the boundless compassion of God for our human situation.

God Is Passionate about Social and Economic Justice

Throughout the Bible God manifests an unmistakable preferential option for the poor. Over the centuries, through prophetic voice after prophetic voice, God makes God's purposes known. God remembers the poor and the marginalized. Over time, kings have a tendency to forget; God remembers. In Amos 6, God is indignant at the injustice of Judah's leaders toward the poor:

> *Woe to those who lie on beds of ivory, and lounge on their couches, and eat lambs from the flock, and calves from the stall; who sing idle songs to the sound of the harp, and like David improvise on instruments of music; who drink wine from bowls, and anoint themselves with the finest oils, but are not grieved over the ruin of Joseph!* (Amos 6:4–6, from RSV)

Amos is forecasting the demise of Judah, the northern kingdom of Israel, which is eventually destroyed by the Assyrians in 722 BCE. About the use of the word *woe* in the Bible, Old Testament scholar Walter Brueggemann used to say: *Woe means, you're going to die.* Amos has a hard word for Judah's leaders, going on to say, "They shall now be the first to go into exile" (Amos 6:7a).

The deepest value of the Christian life is the value of suffering love. *Suffering love* simply means we gotta give up stuff. As human beings, as children of God, we have to share. We have to make sacrifices. We have to look out for the needy, for the less fortunate, for those whose lives have been diminished in whatever way by the turbulent winds of life. Suffering love is what God (the Spirit) calls us to.

In Matthew's gospel, the rich young man in the parable learns a hard lesson. No doubt wanting to exalt himself, he approaches Jesus with a question: "What good deed must I do to have eternal life?" Jesus tells him, "If you wish to enter into life, keep the commandments" (Matthew 19:16, 17). Jesus then identifies some of the most important commandments, whereupon the young man says to Jesus, "I have kept all these; what do I still lack?" (Matthew 19:20). Jesus then says to him:

> *"If you wish to be perfect, go, sell your possessions, and give the money to the poor, and you will have treasure in heaven; then come, follow me." When the young man heard this word, he went away grieving, for he had many possessions.* (Matthew 19:21–22)

Through this poignant parable of Jesus, we see God's passion for social and economic justice vividly manifest. As Christians and seekers, the path of the *Christ way* leads to discovering the need for detachment from all things that captivate us and hinder our ability to live and love freely. That is what suffering love calls us to; it is what God's purposes call us to.

JESUS AND THE CHRISTIAN LIFE

Is Jesus the Messiah?

The term *Messiah* means "the anointed one," as in the anointed one of God. Before the kings of Israel became lost during the period of Babylonian captivity (587–538 BCE), kings themselves were known as the anointed ones of God. By the time of Jesus, a wistful hope had evolved within Judaism for the return of such an anointed one—a Messiah—who would lift Israel again into the promises God held for her. After Jesus' crucifixion, over the years, the evolving post-Easter communities of faith began increasingly to see Jesus in messianic terms. For them, he became the Messiah or, in Greek, *the Christ*.

I have doubts as to whether the pre-Easter Jesus saw himself as the Messiah. Although in Jesus' first-century world, over time, Messiahs had come and gone (usually meeting a violent death), still, it would be a bit much to suggest Jesus saw himself in such exalted terms. At the same time, metaphorically speaking, I do believe that God came to see Jesus as God's Messiah. As the meaning and depth of resurrection unfolded over the months and years in the lives of the early Christian communities, I believe these communities increasingly came to believe God claimed Jesus as God's anointed one. In other words, in their experience, they came to believe that God claimed Jesus' life as a glimpse of what God's life is like.

Simply put, I believe Jesus is God's Messiah. Jesus is the one whom God resurrected, the one through whom a new awareness and new consciousness was born. Jesus is the one who reveals for us the depths of what it means to be human. Jesus is the one who shows us what it means to live a life centered in God, a life full of God. Jesus is the one in whom and through whom the transformative power of suffering love invites us all to deeply human lives of self-giving and love—again, that we may all be one.

Salvation

In our Christian tradition, *salvation* is a loaded, multilayered term. Depending on the way we read the Bible and on how we think about our faith, it means different things to different people. For conservative-evangelical Christians, it is a core element of faith. Generally, conservative-evangelicals want to *know* (feel strongly) they are saved. Having a deeply felt sense they are saved is critical to how they think about their faith; indeed, it is a core element in their identity as Christians. Yet many progressive Christians think about salvation differently. We think of it as a process of becoming whole, a transformative process that redeems our true self—the self that is creative, spontaneous in love and acceptance, and open to mystery, wonder, and awe.

No matter how we think of salvation, it remains elusive. It is not something about which we can claim knowledge or experience. As humans, we cannot *know* it. It is not a happening or event we can control; it is not some final realization we can claim for ourselves or others. At its best, salvation is hope. It is the hope we have in God and in what God has revealed to us in the life, death, and resurrection of Jesus. In this larger sense, ultimately, salvation is God's domain.

In the Bible, there are two macro stories of salvation that give us insight into our biblical understandings of salvation. These stories are *the* two overarching stories of the Hebrew Scriptures: the Exodus and the Exile. Related in metaphorical language, the Exodus (thirteenth century BCE) is the liberation of the Israelites from the oppressive hand of Pharaoh in Egypt. In the story, God hears the cries of Israel and sends Moses to free the Israelites and lead them toward the promised land. This action by God on behalf of Israel becomes *the* core event in Israel's history, an event that, again and again, reminds Israel of God's steadfast love and protection. In Israel's memory, God is *the* God that freed her from the oppressive hand of Pharaoh. Israel's God, therefore, is to be trusted and revered. In the unfolding centuries, Israel's memory of the Exodus experience is forever cemented in her identity as a people. God has indeed *saved* Israel in the Exodus experience.

The Exile (sixth century BCE) was Israel's devastating experience of some fifty years in Babylonian exile. Prompted by her sinful and wayward ways, Israel in exile became an overwhelming experience of shame and alienation, an experience that cut her off from her homeland and her historical sense of who she was in relation to God. The solution—her salvation—would be to return home, a turning away from her wayward past (i.e., a repentance) and a return to Jerusalem and the land of Judah. Although the scope of the return was no doubt notably less than what Israel hoped for, it was nonetheless a return in what is known as the restoration. It was a new beginning, a salvation from her devastation.

Although salvation is biblical, it is not a primary emphasis of the biblical message. The popular notion of salvation in American Christianity is tainted with distortions and problems directly related to conservative-evangelical Christianity's version of Christian faith. For example, in conservative-evangelical churches, generally the goal of the sermon is to prompt "decisions for Christ." The preacher may have other goals as well, but the larger purpose is that those listening to the sermon be moved to "make a decision for Christ." This decision is a profession of belief and faith, all a part of a simple formula for becoming a Christian.

In this formula, a person professes belief in Jesus Christ as Lord and Savior, nodding in the affirmative that he died for our sins and will come again in the Second Coming. The person is then baptized and becomes a part of the body of Christ that is the church, believing his or her salvation is secured in this process.

An initial problem with this notion of salvation is that Christianity is reduced to a religion of requirements. A person only needs to say and do the right thing to be saved. This version of faith exposes another problem as well: it promotes Christianity as an in-group/out-group faith—those who are *in* are saved and those who are *out* are not. More still, this view of salvation places too much emphasis on the next world rather than on transformation in this world.

I do not believe salvation in the Christian faith is related to *right belief* or to some formulaic profession of faith. Rather, salvation is the birth in the human spirit of a new awareness and new consciousness leading to an ongoing process of personal transformation. Beyond this, salvation is also social; it is about making life in this world better. It is not unconcerned about the future; still, its overwhelming focus is on this world, on individual and community life in our everyday experience.

Whatever salvation is, it is the work of God, the work of the Spirit. It is an on-going process. It is not something we can claim for ourselves or for others. Sal-vation is a way of life, a way of being, a way of the Spirit. It is a way of becoming more whole, more healed from our woundedness, more in harmony with the Spirit, and more alive in our relationships.

Again, while the Bible believes in salvation and in the afterlife, it believes more in living lives of ongoing transformation in this world. It believes in living a good life today, in making right choices today, in advocating for peace with social and economic justice today. In the Bible, suffering love is the deepest value. Whatever salvation, heaven, and the afterlife are—however they are understood—they are a consequence of a prior lived-out commitment to suffering love. Suffering love is the way of Jesus. It is the way that prompts each of us to do what we need to do (i.e., to make the necessary sacrifices), that we may all be one.

Heaven, the Afterlife, and Eternal Life

To begin with, as noted before, heaven is *not* an actual place or location. Heaven is a metaphor for an idealized state we go to or enter into when we die. As a metaphor, heaven is a picture we paint to give comfort and reassurance to the bereaved. It is a final resting place for us and our loved ones. The afterlife is related to heaven but is generally not thought of as a place. It is associated with the hope we Christians hold on to on the other side of our dying. Both heaven and the afterlife lift up the hope that, as Christians, we do not die into a void absent of meaning; rather, we die into God, we die into the Spirit.

Biblically, *eternal life* is more accurately understood as "life in the age to come." However we understand it, *eternal life* and *eternity* are noted in the Bible and point to some form of existence beyond death. Heaven, the afterlife, and eternal life are all language we humans have co-opted to give us hope in the face of death. Clearly death and dying are realities we care deeply about as we continue in our struggle to accept them and find ways of reconciling ourselves to them.

Truth be told, we do not know what happens to our spirits when we die. In trying to unpack the deeper meaning of salvation and resurrection, I have talked a lot about how they are experiences of personal transformation. To be saved or resurrected is to have a new awareness and new consciousness that leads to an ongoing personal transformation. It is to give oneself and one's life to the power of suffering love, that we may all be one.

In Paul's writings, he suggests that after we die we are *re-created*. He says it happens in an instant, like the sounding of a trumpet. Trumpet sounding is a tradition in the Hebrew Scriptures signaling an important event or happening, such as a trumpeting to war or the ushering in of a new age. Paul reminds us of this in these vivid words from 1 Corinthians 15:

> *For the trumpet will sound, and the dead will be raised imperishable, and we will be changed. For the perishable body must put on imperishability, and this mortal body must put on immortality.* (1 Corinthians 15:52–53)

In other words, in spirit we are transformed (i.e., changed, re-created) instantly into a spiritual body—and into an imperishability and immortality that is one with God.

Moreover, if we think about the power of God's love and how nothing can separate us from its energy, we come to believe in the transformation that takes place in our dying. By the power of love, we are not separated from God nor from our loved ones:

> *Who will separate us from the love of Christ [or of God]? Will hardship, or distress, or persecution, or famine, or nakedness, or peril, or sword? . . . No, in all these things we are more than conquerors through him who loved us. For I am convinced that neither death, nor life, nor angels, nor rulers, nor things present, nor things to come, nor powers, nor height, nor depth, nor anything else in all creation, will be able to separate us from the love of God in Christ Jesus our Lord.* (Romans 8:35, 37–39)

This reading from Romans 8 is perhaps *the* pinnacle affirmation of Christian faith and belief. Its words and spirit continue to resonate through the ages.

I have always believed the spirit of human beings, as energy, lives on. It lives on in us, the living. And it lives on in the larger Spirit of the universe. I also believe that love, as spirit, lives on. In this sense, upon death, the love we have shared with our loved ones lives on. I like to say it lives on in the larger Spirit of God. When we die, I believe our spirit is united with those whom we have loved most and who have loved us most. At its best, whatever heaven is about— whatever it means—it's about love.

CHRISTIANITY IN AN AGE OF PLURALISM

The best of our Christian faith does not arrogantly claim that Christianity is the only way to God. It does not seek to diminish the faith claims of other religions. When we are at our best as Christians, we are open and welcoming of all religions, all faiths, all ways of experiencing God and the Spirit.

While the religions of the world tend to share much in common (e.g., beliefs about neighborly love, peaceful relations between nations, etc.), they are not all the same. It is not a question of one religion being superior. All religions have their unique qualities depending on their historical and geographical context. In our modern age of religious pluralism, it is important that we are tolerant and respectful of other religions as we seek to live out our faith amidst the increasing diversity of our evolving world.

So why am I Christian? To state it plainly, I am Christian because that is the faith God has given me. I was born into a Christian family and a Christian context. I could have been born in another part of the world and grown up in a totally different religious context. With a different personal story I could easily have been Jewish, Muslim, or Hindu. Again, Christianity is the faith God has given me. It is the faith I was born into.

Why Be Christian?

At its best, Christianity has a wonderful message to offer the world. Rooted in the suffering love of Jesus, Christian faith teaches that we all have to give up stuff. We all have to make sacrifices on behalf of the whole—on behalf of the family, the team, the group, the office, the church, the community, the nation, and the planet. The best of Christianity unveils a big spirit, a spirit that respects individual differences and welcomes diversity of all kinds.

At its best, Christianity offers a powerful vision for peace on the planet. With the memory of Good Friday at the center of our faith, we are compelled to behold the cross and to remember the reality and transformative power of suffering love. As we remember, we are challenged to turn away from whatever darkness might be in our spirits and to open ourselves, with courage and purpose, to neighborly love and lives of peace with justice for all God's people.

While lauding the virtues of Christian faith, regrettably, we have to also acknowledge that at its worst, there are always some people claiming to be Christian (pastors and other believers) who border on the demonic in some of the things they say and do.

I am writing a couple years after the abhorrent massacre of forty-nine innocent people (mostly gays) at the Pulse bar in Orlando, Florida. As despicable and ugly as this mass shooting was, almost as reprehensible were the sermons of two right-wing, fundamentalist pastors (one in Sacramento and the other in Arizona) announcing to their congregations their regret that more gays had not been murdered (based on a literal and incorrect reading of Leviticus 18). To their demented minds, in the name of Christ, all gays and lesbians should be rounded up and executed. Their evil pronouncements are a reminder of how the best and the worst of the human spirit are revealed through the passions of religion.

Dark voices exist in all religions, and, of course, these voices are at most a radical minority. Still, as Christian communities we have to continue to rise up against such perverse distortions of our faith. A progressive, emerging Christianity compels us to hold fast to the love that is always the heartbeat of our faith story—the love that Paul spoke of, the love that *"bears all things, believes all things, hopes all things and endures all things*, [the] love that *never ends"* (1 Corinthians 13:7–8a). It is the depth and power of this love that beckons us to the spiritual high ground of God's purposes.

Why Be a Church Person?

Although I am not always happy with the church on many levels, still, I am an ardent church person. What is it about the church that I find appealing and meaningful?

To begin with, I like being a part of a church community that is hopefully diverse, where we come together every week (or when the Spirit moves) to meet God and to live out together our faith traditions. I like being a part of Christian celebrations of Advent, Christmas, Thanksgiving, Lent, Easter, and Pentecost. Celebrations of these holy days give meaning and purpose to my life. Even more, I like celebrating these traditions with my family.

I like being a part of a Christian community that celebrates the sacred observances of Baptism, Confirmation, Marriage, and memorial services when we die. Being with people—family, for sure, but friends too—during these very personal and sacred occasions is special beyond words. Memories abound of these sacred occasions, times when we feel a special closeness to God, the Spirit, and loved ones.

And I like being a part of a church where the hope of a fresh word from God always hovers on the horizon. I like to be inspired. We never know how the Spirit might move in the heart, mind, and spirit of the preacher. We never know when a word might be spoken that I need to hear, or when a word might be proclaimed that inspires me and lifts me to a new understanding of God's designs and God's ways. The possibility of fresh inspiration and insight always exists.

Finally, I like being a church person because, at its best, the church stands for and proclaims a message of hope. It is a hope profoundly embedded in the biblical story and in the life, death, and resurrection of Jesus. It is the hope that reassures us as Christians and that nudges us always to embrace the future with promise.

HOPE IN THE CHRISTIAN VISION FOR LIFE

The power and appeal of Christian faith emerges from the hope Christianity brings to the world and to our common human experience. Always, Christianity calls us to hope. At the core of this hope is the suffering love of Jesus. Suffering love is the highest value of Christian faith. It is *the* love that invites each of us to become a bigger person with a more welcoming, more inclusive spirit, so that we may all be one. It is *the* love God dreams about for every human being, every family, every community, every nation, and for all of creation.

What I have tried to show in this book is how the best of the Bible, God, and Jesus offer tremendous hope for the world. When we allow the Bible to breathe, which means when we read the Bible in light of its historical context and primarily as metaphorical narrative, the timeless teachings and wisdom of the Bible become for us a sacrament of the sacred. They speak to the depths of our spirit. They nurture us and guide us in our relentless quest to live meaningful lives.

SCRIPTURE INDEX

Christian Scriptures

INDEX